THE REAL
LEONARDO DA VINCI

To those who are not scared of experimenting, trying new things and going after what they want wholeheartedly.

THE REAL
LEONARDO
DA VINCI

Rose Sgueglia

PEN & SWORD
HISTORY

AN IMPRINT OF PEN & SWORD BOOKS LTD.
YORKSHIRE – PHILADELPHIA

First published in Great Britain in 2021 by
PEN AND SWORD HISTORY
An imprint of
Pen & Sword Books Ltd
Yorkshire – Philadelphia

ISBN 978 1 52676 105 7

A CIP catalogue record for this book is available from the British Library.

Typeset in Times New Roman 11.5/14 by
SJmagic DESIGN SERVICES, India.
Printed and bound by CPI Group (UK) Ltd, Croydon, CR0 4YY

Pen & Sword Books Limited incorporates the imprints of Atlas, Archaeology,
Aviation, Discovery, Family History, Fiction, History, Maritime, Military, Military
Classics, Politics, Select, Transport, True Crime, Air World, Frontline Publishing,
Leo Cooper, Remember When, Seaforth Publishing, The Praetorian Press,
Wharncliffe Local History, Wharncliffe Transport, Wharncliffe True Crime and
White Owl.

For a complete list of Pen & Sword titles please contact
PEN & SWORD BOOKS LIMITED
47 Church Street, Barnsley, South Yorkshire, S70 2AS, England
E-mail: enquiries@pen-and-sword.co.uk
Website: www.pen-and-sword.co.uk

Or
PEN AND SWORD BOOKS
1950 Lawrence Rd, Havertown, PA 19083, USA
E-mail: Uspen-and-sword@casematepublishers.com
Website: www.penandswordbooks.com

Contents

Acknowledgements

Thank you to the team at Pen & Sword for all their help and support.

Thank you to film director Jesus Garces Lambert for talking to me about his beautiful film, *Io Leonardo*.

Thank you to the press office at Sky Arte for being so professional, supportive and wonderful during such a challenging time.

Thank you to Lucky Red, Fabio Zayed and Maila Iacovelli for letting me use their beautiful pictures from *Io Leonardo*.

Thank you to writer, researcher, founder and president of Comitato nazionale per la valorizzazione dei beni storici, culturali e ambientali, Silvano Vinceti, for taking the time to answer my questions about his findings concerning the *Mona Lisa*.

A special thank you goes to my sister for taking care of literally everything else while I finished this book.

Thank you to my family.

And finally, thank you to my friends for all your virtual hugs during COVID-19.

Preface

I finished writing this book during the COVID-19 crisis. One day we were in work, gathering in groups of more than fifty, the next not so much, then not at all.

The last public gathering I went to was a concert at the end of February in Cardiff with my sister, a surreal experience, right before everything kicked off. Leonardo was my little anchor and escaping to the Renaissance the only possible vacation from lockdown.

During those long months, I had the chance to go on a challenging yet incredibly rewarding trip. I took the time to visit a different Florence, an open-minded, artistic, libertine Florence. I soared over Milan where I imagined what it would have been like living at the court of Ludovico Sforza and then I stayed with the infamous Borgia family for a bit, where I almost feared for my life.

It was a no-passport adventure and all happening through the pages of this book, but certainly the experience of a lifetime. Leonardo was my companion; trustworthy, loyal Leonardo who did not like injustice and was there for his friends.

I learnt about him by looking at his beautiful paintings, really looking at what he did, and what a sublime artist he was. I found out about his mysteries, his love for learning, and I read his notebooks, about his inventions. It comes as no surprise that he was a talented man.

Far from being only the wise man with a long beard and what could only be described as prophetic eyes, who always kept looking at the future and never stayed too much in the present, Leonardo was incredibly human; particularly so in his ways of approaching his work, his relationships and his passions.

I found an insecure genius who could paint beautifully but who would also leave most things unfinished and still, today, I am not 100 per cent sure why.

Leonardo gave me a little breather from lockdown, COVID-19 and the incertitude of it all. We got close. He was a writer, yet not an emotional one – he was a man of science. I found a man who had been missing love, from his parents, from his family, a man who tried to fill a void by learning about everyone, about everything, as much as he could.

I researched his life, his iconic reputation and why people still cannot seem to get tired of him. He is present in what we do and he is everywhere we look. He is the *Mona Lisa*, he is the 'maestro', he is the innovator, the myth, the legend and the icon.

He is so many things, yet here I am showing who he is to me. Here's my real Leonardo.

Chapter 1

Leonardo da Vinci, the Underdog

This is the fierce stare of someone who cannot and will not be tamed. The fatal shot is now gone, the warrior stands tall, the head of his opponent at his feet. He is handsome, young but above all, he is luminous, a 'celestial' being in the making. 'Look at me,' he is saying, 'I won, no one expected me to but I did, me with my light but chiselled figure, me with the recklessness of my years, that lack of experience, education perhaps, me with only the power of my wit, now bow down to my victory, bow down to me, David, Leonardo, the underdog.'

The arrogance of youth, the beauty and a smile that tells it all. It's a legendary story that unravels before our eyes and probably one of the greatest masterpieces we will ever see by sculptor Andrea del Verrocchio: the bronze statue of David succeeds in distinguishing itself by many aspects but, most importantly, it surely has the merit of showing a more realistic version of the well-known story. It perhaps still stands today as one of the closest representations to the original.

Verrocchio's *David* is beautiful, athletic, flawless to many but it's not the muscular, bulky figure we have grown accustomed to through the work of other artists in the history of the art world. Compared to other representations of David, and granted that most of them came after Verrocchio's personal interpretation, Verrocchio's statue is almost fully clothed and holds a sword, carelessly.

Yes, he is armed, but this David needs no arms to make him the man that he really is. In order to kill Goliath, he has been graced with unstoppable gifts no one else seems to have; it's in his agility, in his brain, in his beauty and, of course, in his speed that this biblical hero is capable of finding the key to finally kill the giant.

The head of Goliath, far from lying between his feet, is positioned directly under David's right foot, a little trick which magisterially manages to maintain the balance of the composition; the beauty and

1

the difference, if not the originality, of Verrocchio's statue is vivid and present in David's expression, as this turns out to be of a young, provocative, gorgeous lad who smirks at the audience.

Verrocchio's *David* is still a man, a young man, and this man tells us a story, unravelling a double narrative we are not necessarily prepared to listen to, perhaps not yet; at first, it's biblical, the plot is simple yet layered. We all know the fable of a young, mighty, foxy shepherd named David who fights the giant Goliath and wins, triumphs despite doubters.

The narrative is simple; it stands there, right by David's feet, and culminates in Goliath's head, a symbol of victory. It's modern, too modern in fact – the David/Goliath story has, after all, become a metaphor for life, and even Verrocchio knows that. He is fully aware that in order to make his reinterpretation different and to finally make sure it stands out in one way or another, making his statue something people will remember for a very long time, he needs to give David an upgrade. It is almost like Verrocchio knows David intimately.

David is an underdog, someone who dares to challenge someone else or something bigger, taller, smarter or just more favoured by the world than he ever will be.

David is the underdog who wins, becoming legend instead; now everyone will know who he is, everyone will know his name and everyone will sing his praises, talk about his adventures and use his example for the years and centuries to come. Verrocchio knows one particular underdog, someone who will be the perfect model for his statue, a man who wasn't born under the most favourable circumstances yet who has this talent, this light, this beauty; a young man, by many considered gorgeous, tall, intelligent, slightly arrogant, just a sign of his youth, but someone who has so many talents and possibilities, someone different, special perhaps and someone who goes by the name of Leonardo, known to everyone else as Leonardo da Vinci.

Leonardo da Vinci was born on 15 April 1452, in Anchiano, a little village in the Florentine area known for its beautiful landscapes and sweet hills which had the merit of inspiring his genius and keeping a strong hold on him throughout his life. Leonardo was born, according to many biographers and researchers, in a small cottage where he spent very little time, as originally the family was from Vinci. That is where little Leonardo ended up spending most of his childhood, surrounded by nature, which turned out to be his very first and perhaps most loved teacher.

A small town in the heart of Tuscany, Vinci stood right in the middle of the hills of Montalbano, taking its proud and rightful place between Pistoia, Prato and Florence and dating back to the early Middle Ages when it was previously ruled by the Guidi counts, a famous Italian family originally from the region of Romagna. During the tenth century, the Guidi counts had control over different regions in the Florentine area including Vinci.

Leonardo was the illegitimate son of a local and well-known notary called Ser Piero and a woman called Caterina. Caterina was a servant, someone who did not hold a pioneering role in Leonardo's life, and who was a blurry figure in his story, someone who rarely appeared in his writing.

We don't have much information about her but we know that she was from a poor family herself and was pressured to marry another man in haste, shortly after Leonardo's birth.

Leonardo's stepfather, Attaccabriga, which in Italian means trouble-maker (although, apparently, he wasn't one), did not seem overly concerned with Caterina's situation. They married quickly, and together they went on to have several other children as part of their newly created family, forgetting soon about Leonardo but leaving him in the capable hands of his grandparents and uncle. It was almost as if he had never existed in his mother's life.

Many biographers have speculated on the circumstances surrounding Leonardo's birth. It would not have been unusual for the time for Leonardo to have been a product of violence and rape, especially considering how legitimised the act was at that time, but no one has ever confirmed or denied such a claim, and even Leonardo himself, who hardly spoke about his personal life, never mentioned anything about the matter, keeping a discreet silence over his mother and family.

Only later, in his notebooks, did he clearly express his thoughts, finally voicing his personal beliefs concerning violence against women and rape in particular, never in a clear way but using a different topic to perhaps illustrate his most hidden thoughts. The notes he made in his notebooks mostly concerned the personality and the nature of a child and how it could be influenced by external factors from the very beginning. He thought that parents could be responsible for their child's nature. He believed that children who were the product of rape could lack positive characteristics including being lovable, lively and witty.

In these notes, Leonardo does not fully express himself concerning whether he had been a product of love or if he had been the ultimate result of violence. Yet it is at this time in his life that he finally talks, shares his thoughts about love, something he did rarely, especially when it came to sexual love. Leonardo does not only freely express his beliefs but also gives us a revolutionary concept for the time: maybe for the first time in history, someone starts considering women as equal to men, at least when it comes to sex; women, according to Leonardo, need to play an active part when it comes to pleasure. This is vital, according to him, to give birth to happy, lively and lovable children, who are ready for this world.

According to Kia Vahland, author of *The Da Vinci Women: The Untold Feminist Power of Leonardo's Art*, the concept of love was still quite new for the Renaissance period, an era when most marriages were pre-arranged and prostitution was widespread. Financial reasons and even status issues were an important factor most people had to account for when deciding to marry someone or even just start courting. Yet the Renaissance period, according to Vahland, was a time where love was highly represented, promoted and longed for in any form of art from visual art to literature, performances and pictures. It was a great, constant celebration that was largely influenced by the strong presence and power of the Medici family in Florence.

In her work, Vahland mentions that in order to secure their power and not be replaced by other Italian families who were just as wealthy and not happy about the Medici and their ascension to power, the Medici planned a big tournament in Piazza Santa Croce which had the double effect of cementing their supremacy and also rekindling their alliance with Venice and Milan. This eventually helped them contrast and protect their sovereignty from the other families, most of them from the South of Italy.

Love was not an easy topic for Leonardo. Despite being everywhere in Florence, despite the songs, the art, the culture and the concept of romantic courtship becoming an important element in everyday life during the Renaissance, he was never very interested in love, particularly romantic or sexual love.

From his childhood, or just by considering his background, love was not something that Leonardo had strongly experienced, in particular from his mother or his mother's side of the family. He had never felt protected, loved or taken care of by a maternal figure and once Caterina was married with other children, four girls and a boy, he grew even more detached from that part of his family.

Caterina didn't pay much attention to her firstborn, and despite most biographers speculating about Leonardo spending time between both his mother's and his father's families equally, it was the latter which became Leonardo's childhood home, the family he would eventually recognise as such. Leonardo's father's family, particularly his grandfather Antonio and his wife, became for him something that would support him and help him grow in this initial stage of his life. He would spend endless days playing in his grandfather's house with close, intimate contact with nature. He was particularly attached to his grandfather and to his uncle, Francesco, who was only fifteen years older than Leonardo; the two had a strong bond and he was fundamental in Leonardo's upbringing. They shared a love for the countryside and often spent entire days together. They were so close that Francesco was mistaken by several biographers as Leonardo's father.

Caterina's absence from Leonardo's life, notes or paintings became bigger than any other presence. They were never together, hardly ever lived in the same house and only had the chance to reconnect when, after Leonardo's stepfather's death, Caterina, now elderly, widowed and unable to take care of herself, went to live with Leonardo. This was carefully written by Leonardo in his notes; in one of the passages he wrote about his mother, Leonardo carefully lists all the expenses he had to make for Caterina's funeral when, not even a month after moving with her eldest son, she passed away. The tone of his notes was cold, almost detached. He called her 'La Caterina' and never 'mother', advancing several hypotheses that claim that Caterina was not Leonardo's mother in the first place.

Several researchers have criticised Leonardo and his notes; many have particularly condemned the fact that he didn't seem to spend enough money for the funeral itself, others say that he would usually spend much more on clothes, stressing Leonardo's passion for fashion and how much he liked to always be dressed appropriately for every occasion.

Other researchers argue that 123 soldi, the sum Leonardo spent on her funeral, was just not enough for someone who was supposed to be so close and dear to him, at least by blood, speculating that Caterina was just someone working for him, a servant. The list of Leonardo's expenses for Caterina's funeral featured as part of his notes in the Codex Forster notebook and the expenses included medical fees, wax for candles, four priests, the bells, the gravediggers and four altar boys.

However, a note from the State Archives of Milan confirmed Caterina's death from malaria, and despite the note misspelling Caterina's name, calling her Chaterina, it is widely accepted that she was the same woman who gave birth to Leonardo.

Caterina was an enigmatic character in Leonardo's life, a detached figure, the origin of all Leonardo's trouble for Freud and the beginning of that intrinsic solitude he felt all his life, according to many. A profound detachment from his mother and his mother's new family with Attaccabriga pushed Leonardo even closer to his father and his side of the family. Ser Piero, Leonardo's father, had no other children and would not have others until Leonardo was 24. Leonardo grew closer to his father and it was because of him that he began considering visual art as a potential career.

His paternal relationship, the love he had for his father and the constant search for his approval, had, in fact, the merit of creating the perfect conditions for the next new phase in Leonardo's life: Florence.

Chapter 2

Leonardo, the Florentine Man

By the time he was 12, Leonardo was a young man who had to find employment and a purpose in life. Like most teenagers of the time, he needed to be independent and learn a profession to become self-sufficient. He was a curious lad, ready to learn, eager to find himself, and that is why, following the death of his beloved grandfather, he left Vinci and his childhood to move to Florence and finally embrace adulthood.

It must not have been easy for a young Leonardo to let go of everything he knew – Vinci, the place he had grown attached to, those hills he loved, those landscapes, the general feeling of peace he only experienced in his father's family home surrounded by those who loved him, cared for him and spent time understanding his whole being. Vinci was home and everything that he held dear; it must have given him some level of anxiety, at such a young age, to leave everything behind, experiencing grief for the first time as well. The pain from the death of his grandfather and his stepmother, Piero's second wife, who had died around the same time in childbirth, gave him just enough strength to take a leap of faith and embrace a new life far from everything he had ever known, a new life in Florence.

Despite the trauma of having to leave everything behind, there is almost no trace of that pain in his notes, and that is something that is a recurrent theme in Leonardo's writing, despite the strong, at times nervous, emotional pace he usually conferred on his creative writing work and even his paintings, his works of art. Leonardo was always a little shy and discreet when it came to talking or being open about his own emotions. He was very scientific in the way he analysed and expressed feelings, almost as though he was interested in why he was feeling the way he was but not so much in lingering in it or even feeling emotions, to avoid being completely overwhelmed by it.

Despite having to leave what he knew behind, Florence represented an opportunity, and Leonardo would never shy away from opportunities, especially those which could potentially change and challenge him the most, no matter how scary they were.

Florence represented something that would improve his being, give him that sense of purpose he was already looking for, or maybe concretise what he already had in mind, what he already knew he could do, perhaps better than anyone else. As a young boy, Leonardo had already shown a strong partiality to visual art and art in general, which was mostly connected to his appreciation for nature and his surroundings. He was a keen observer of life, nature and people and he managed to successfully express that from the beginning and with very little education.

At 12 years old, knowing that he could not follow his father's footsteps and embrace a legal career – he was, after all, an illegitimate son – he joined Ser Piero in Florence, where he was urged to find a job.

That is how he quickly became an apprentice and started working at a very famous workshop in Florence, one belonging to painter Andrea del Verrocchio. Piero had noticed Leonardo taking an interest in sketching and drawing and, feeling responsible for his firstborn's future, despite Leonardo being born out of wedlock, he had decided to take the matter into his own hands and bring Leonardo's early works to Verrocchio. He did not have any expectations; perhaps he just appreciated the famous painter and sculptor taking some time to have a look at his son's work and establish whether a career as a painter could be the right path for Leonardo as well.

At the time, Verrocchio had a strong reputation in Florence, and many admired him for his work. He was a sculptor and a painter and was extremely well known during the Renaissance era; he was also the first to recognise in Leonardo something valid and important. After having a look at Leonardo's early works, it is reported that Verrocchio was so touched by their quality and beauty that he insisted on having him work for him as part of his team of young apprentices at his workshop in Florence. Despite his young age, Leonardo was more advanced than other artists before him; he had a technique not many had, and proved to be much more talented than anyone who had or had not received any formal education. It was perhaps the absence of a formal education that had forged Leonardo's mind and nurtured his multiple interests.

As it turned out, being born out of wedlock had its advantages: Leonardo could do what he wanted with his life, experience his passions and take the direction he fancied the most. Being an illegitimate son, Leonardo did not have to become a notary like his father (not that he had any interest in a legal career anyway), something that was custom for the firstborn male in a wealthy family, and did not have to go to Latin school.

Despite this, nothing would have given Leonardo more happiness than being recognised by his father and have the chance to study, not necessarily in preparation for a legal position but perhaps other subjects. He had a curious personality; he was someone who was interested in learning and finding out about everything, and for years to come he tried to compensate for that lack of education by learning as much as he could every single day. There was something missing in him that had not been completely fulfilled during his childhood years.

Not going to Latin school and not receiving a formal education had a strong impact on him for the rest of his life; he tried hard to teach himself what he had missed out on but sometimes with scarce results, especially when it came to Latin.

He tried to learn Latin on his own later in life, and many notebooks have been found with him practising his Latin words, but many biographers believe that he never succeeded or perhaps that he never had a true interest, as most of his notebooks have been found to be written in Italian. Leonardo was also famous for leaving things unfinished and, despite the initial enthusiasm, he would usually leave new projects aside, losing interest. He left paintings, often commissioned and already paid for, incomplete; many believed that it was due to a lack of focus.

He certainly boasted a level of freedom, doing as he pleased, which many people born under legitimised circumstances did not have. There were literally no expectations when it came to him, and what a relief that must have been.

Being born out of wedlock was fairly common in Italy during the Renaissance, especially within the upper, wealthier classes but not so much, as it turns out, with middle-class people, who preferred to keep a much more dignified presence and had more standardised unions and relationships.

In her book, *Visibilis et Invisibilis: The Mistress in Italian Renaissance Court Society*, Helen S. Ettlinger talks about the Renaissance being considered the 'golden age for bastards' and 'the age of golden bastards'. She writes about how illicit relationships were the norm during the Renaissance and how they were often sought by families in order to gain favours and boast of a better influence as part of the society of the time. Often, husbands would offer their wives to important men of power for personal and family gains.

As a consequence of this, Italy saw an increase in pregnancies out of wedlock, something which was not necessarily considered a reason for public humiliation. At this time in history, women had few rights and the figure of the mistress had a tendency to stay in the shadows, sometimes only being recognised after giving birth.

Circumstances changed, and giving birth to children outside wedlock largely depended on the social status of the woman. As stressed by several researchers, being a mistress didn't necessarily mean a lower position in society, and many women who were already married, or belonging to wealthy families, would also be mistresses of important men, and their wealth and social position would also influence their children born in or out of wedlock.

Leonardo's mother was not a member of a wealthy family and was quickly married off to someone else; it would not be completely wrong to assume that perhaps it had not been her choice to give birth to a child outside of wedlock. She was not high in the society of the time and she had no interest in being closer to powerful men for personal gains, and that is probably why Leonardo's position was in no way a favourable one to start with. Despite this, having no other children of his own, Leonardo's father and paternal family took an interest in the child and did whatever they could to support his upbringing, first in Vinci and then in Florence.

In many ways, maybe without him even realising, Leonardo had the best of both worlds; he had access to many of the connections of his father's side of the family, growing closer to his paternal grandparents as well as his father's new family and stepmother, while also succeeding in maintaining a detachment which culminated in Leonardo being able to express himself creatively by exploring his talent and living off his art.

The absence of a forced, imposed, archaic education also helped Leonardo to develop an inquisitive mind, being left free to explore his surroundings, and in many ways to look at the world and the nature around him from a much more refreshing, curious and experimental perspective, something which he didn't forget and always brought with him wherever he went and whatever project he was working on.

He loved to say that before trying anything new, including starting a new project or giving life to a new concept, even only in his head, a work of art, sculpture or invention, he liked to test, give himself the time to understand the dynamics of whatever he was creating, and properly experiment with his ideas, moving any thought from creativity to practicality; something that further proved how much of a scientist rather than a purely creative artist he really was.

One of the most interesting passages in his notebooks that notably expresses his curious personality and his inquisitive mind is the one where he describes entering a dark cave and discovering a whale fossil. It is interesting to see how torn he was between fear and curiosity and how, in the end, he had just decided to give it a go, to forget about his fear and how dark the cave was. Dragged by his own insatiable love for learning and discovering something new, he found the courage to enter the cave and make a fascinating scientific discovery. Many researchers have been careful when it comes to this passage in Leonardo's notes; some believe it to be made up and that the cave never really existed, others have ventured a philosophical explanation with the cave acting as some sort of metaphor. Despite this, several years later, many fossilised whale bones were unveiled in Tuscany.

It was in this continuous search for something, something that he needed to learn, something that he needed in order to fill a void which had been left by the absence of education in his early years, by a mother who was not wealthy and lacked influence, that Leonardo found the courage to move to Florence and meet one of the first men who would change his life, Andrea del Verrocchio.

A leading artist of the late fifteenth century, Andrea del Verrocchio was a sculptor and a painter who was widely celebrated and appreciated, particularly for supporting and having as students some of the most important artists of the time, including, of course, Leonardo.

After training as a goldsmith, Verrocchio started as an artist, but having several prestigious students working at his studio did not help his career. It has been difficult for researchers to establish and recognise some of Verrocchio's works, as several have been manipulated or copied by his just as famous students; as a consequence of this, not many works have been fully attributed to him. Despite a small but important contribution by Leonardo himself, the only work which carries Verrocchio's signature style is *The Baptism of Christ*, currently in the Uffizi in Florence. The rest of his works show some marginal contribution, if not a large part of the work, done or completed by some of his famous students, which included not only Leonardo but also Pietro Perugino, Lorenzo di Credi and even Sandro Botticelli, who studied with Verrocchio during the 1480s. Yet, despite having several famous students at his workshop, Verrocchio also managed to be a pioneering figure himself, inspiring students with his research on new media and different drawing techniques.

In Florence, Verrocchio was famous for being a favourite with the Medici family, the Italian family that ruled Florence and then the rest of Tuscany from 1434 to 1737. It was for the Medici that Verrocchio sculpted a bust of Giuliano de' Medici to mark his birthday, which was celebrated with a jousting contest. Originally, the bust was meant to be painted and completed with several decorations, including a helmet in metal.

Working with the Medici had the benefit of inspiring Verrocchio as he worked under such creative, positive patronage. The Medici supported the arts including painting, sculpture and architecture, which enriched the city of Florence and its habitants and artists alike. It is during this time that the Medici decided to give Verrocchio his most important commission yet, the statue of David with the Head of Goliath, which used Leonardo as the model for David. Later he was also awarded the commission for the bronze group of Christ and Saint Thomas, the tomb of Giovanni and Piero de' Medici, the Cardinal Niccolò Forteguerri Monument, and the famous Equestrian Monument to Bartolomeo Colleoni in Venice.

An interesting episode, which perfectly explained the relationship between Leonardo and Verrocchio is the one which occurred during the production of *The Baptism of Christ*.

As Verrocchio was ready to complete perhaps one of his most famous paintings, Leonardo surprised him, according to many, with a little addition to Verrocchio's work, which took the shape of a beautiful angel. Other versions describe a different situation, in which it was Verrocchio who insisted on Leonardo adding something to his painting, a little touch. As it turns out, Verrocchio was already in awe of Leonardo, and despite his young age, he was absolutely adamant that Leonardo must add something to his painting, on that same canvas. Little did he expect such a dazzling final result.

The Baptism of Christ was commissioned by the monks of San Salvi near Florence, and it is a close representation of the reports found in the gospels of Matthew, Mark and Luke. The scene is simple and well known: John the Baptist pours water over Christ's head while the hands of God come down from the sky and a dove symbolises the Holy Spirit. All four figures share similar characteristics while the angel, the one Leonardo decided or was asked to add, manages to stand out from the rest. The angel has the merit of perfectly embodying some of Leonardo's most famous painting traits, including the beauty of his light hair and the smart, sweet expression of his figures. The draping of the angel's clothes is also something that would become Leonardo's trademark in other works including *The Annunciation*, while the grass by the angel is also a reminder of Leonardo's love and understanding of nature and its beauty.

Compared to Verrocchio's flat figures, Leonardo's angel was characterised by different light and dynamics, and, by looking directly at Jesus, the angel also succeeded in directing the viewer's attention to Jesus, adding balance and perspective to the painting. In his biography, Vasari, who had written about Leonardo and was fascinated by his persona, despite having never met him, noted, as he wrote about his early upbringing and his apprenticeship at Verrocchio's studio, that after seeing Leonardo's angel and how he stood out compared to his own figures, for such grace and perfection, Verrocchio found it so difficult to pick up a brush again that he decided not to paint anymore. Many researchers have labelled this story by Vasari as a legend; Verrocchio was fully aware of Leonardo's talent from the very beginning. However, it is true that *The Baptism of Christ* is one of his last paintings.

Despite Leonardo being considered as a highly superior and more refined painter than Verrocchio ever was, it is also important to acknowledge that it was thanks to Verrocchio and the inspiration he conferred to his students at his workshop that Leonardo fully started to express himself and it was during this time, while he was working with Verrocchio, that Leonardo produced even more works of art, inspired perhaps by the time he spent with his teacher. At this time in his life, he worked on four different paintings, which included a portrait of Ginevra de Benci, two paintings of the Madonna and Child, and *The Annunciation*.

The Annunciation is one of the earliest works by Leonardo and it has been defined as a not fully developed Leonardo because of how early it was created and how less advanced the technique of his painting was; at the time, Leonardo was in his twenties and still quite inexperienced. Yet, despite being one of the first works of art ever produced by him, *The Annunciation* is one of the most important pieces in his early collections. The painting almost effortlessly depicts the moment the Archangel Gabriel, on the left, 'announces' the birth of Jesus Christ to the Virgin Mary, standing on the right, an important moment which Leonardo chooses to portray in what has been considered a very early version of his trademark style.

Leonardo's figures are dynamic. The angel almost seems to have a tridimensional shape thanks to how his clothes fold; it's a trait with which Leonardo had already experimented in Verrocchio's *The Baptism of Christ*. In *The Annunciation*, the angel also looks youthful, especially in comparison with the Virgin Mary, who has also often been defined as appearing cold and a little detached: not only at the news of the Annunciation but also at her surroundings.

Many have also argued that the angel is painted as a creature in full movement, almost in motion. Far from being just beautiful, it also perfectly conveys the idea that he has only just landed, with his wings almost birdlike, another element which has been at the core of Leonardo's studies, giving the idea of movement and providing an early proof of Leonardo's tireless research when it came to birds and their flying. *The Annunciation* follows Leonardo's partiality to narrative development; it's a painting that tells a story, and also reinterprets a well-known story which takes a different direction, thanks to Leonardo's details, pace and movement. Leonardo's version almost becomes personal to him, it is a story, it brings onto canvas all the things he probably loved the most: nature, pace and well-rounded characters.

As he lands, the angel seems to have surprised the Virgin Mary; she raises her finger, a little taken aback, hardly concerned by this majestic figure descending or having just descended before her own eyes. The angel has interrupted her reading, she is about to turn the page and close the book. She is now ready to give her full attention to the messenger and listen to his news.

Even at this early stage, you can tell Leonardo was interested in establishing a conversation between characters in his paintings. His figures are never flat, never acting the way you would expect them to; the Virgin Mary's expression is detached but not closed, the angel is beautiful but not completely divine, he almost moves, even his wings look like they are in full motion; he has just arrived. It is Leonardo alone who is capable of establishing this narrative, this conversation. It is almost a whispered conversation you can hear unravelling; you can listen to the angel and the Virgin Mary having a chat, the same chat they have had in many other paintings and other forms of media, yet it does feel different this time, it does feel bolder, almost more human.

You can also almost feel the wind as it touches the angel's wings; you cannot help but be slightly distracted by the nature surrounding the scene, a beautiful natural scene with green mountain scenery, ever present in Leonardo and his works.

In *The Annunciation*, nature has the power to steal the scene. The main character is not the angel or the Virgin Mary but the garden; the scene is, in fact, fully immersed in nature, which distracts the viewer from the main Catholic, religious message, perhaps something orchestrated on purpose by Leonardo himself.

When he worked on *The Annunciation*, Leonardo was still a young painter, and it is interesting to note that despite already having a strong style, something which he succeeded in expanding and including in all his works, he was also inspired by Verrocchio in different ways, including the theme of the painting he chose to work on.

Verrocchio himself used to paint and work on different religious paintings; choosing a similar theme was a symbol of Leonardo's inspiration and a homage to his teacher.

Many believe that despite *The Annunciation* being a strong starting point in Leonardo's career, it was not as perfect as some of his later works, particularly when it comes to its technique. Many researchers have noted how one of the arms of the Virgin Mary is longer than the other, for example. According to many, this was proof that, despite being a great painter, even Leonardo was still learning how to be Leonardo, and how to reach that level of perfection in his works.

The Annunciation is not the only early work by Leonardo. Another one that has fascinated and interested researchers and media alike for its beauty and technique is the portrait of a woman, Ginevra de Benci.

In the Ginevra de Benci painting, Leonardo expressed his full yet early potential when it came to portrait painting. This is one of the first portraits Leonardo ever finished and the way he succeeds in portraying Ginevra has the merit of bringing something new to Renaissance portrait painting. Leonardo portrays a young Ginevra candidly with perfect features and an almost unapproachable, difficult to understand expression; Ginevra was what researchers have often described as a standard beauty for the time, yet her portrait shows her with superior dignity, another important trait for the women of the period who had to carry themselves with a certain level of modesty no matter what activity they were doing, as their reputation was highly valued, especially as that would have made them more likely to marry well.

At the time of her portrait, Ginevra was 16 years old and came from one of the most important families in Florence, the Benci. The Benci were extremely well known, and it was not rare for women coming from the wealthiest families to boast a great position in the society of the time and an invaluable education. Ginevra was no different, and she was well known and appreciated for her love of poetry and the ability to hold brilliant conversations. The portrait of Ginevra de Benci was most likely commissioned by Luigi Niccolini, her betrothed, in 1474.

At the time of the portrait by Leonardo, Ginevra and Niccolini were courting and the latter perhaps saw fit to start courting this beautiful, highly sought woman with a portrait by the great Leonardo, who was quickly starting to get some recognition within his circle. However, despite being in a serious committed relationship with Niccolini, Ginevra was no stranger to grandiose gestures in her name; she had many admirers who, according to several researchers, ended up proving their love to the beautiful young girl by even composing poetry in her honour. These were often powerful men and included the likes of Lorenzo de' Medici and Bernardo Bembo, who was at the time the Venetian ambassador to Florence. Many researchers and biographers believed that it was not Niccolini but Bembo who commissioned Leonardo to do a painting of his loved one.

The painting was different to anything anyone had ever conceived, and revolutionary for different reasons; Ginevra was painted so perfectly, almost immaculately, that it conferred on the painting an almost lifelike style. The painting also broke the early Renaissance tradition that required women to pose in a more appealing, almost flirtatious way. During the Renaissance period, women were constantly asked to be feminine, appealing to a male audience, something that clearly started to find its opposition in Leonardo's portraits. Ginevra appears to be detached and cold rather than flirtatious; it is almost as though she doesn't want her portrait to be painted. As usual, Leonardo broke with convention; perhaps by accident or maybe it was perfectly orchestrated and dictated by his revolutionary nature. By giving Ginevra the chance to be different, he also gave her a personality, a boldness few other women whose portrait had been painted before her had ever had. Despite giving Ginevra the traits she had been famous and appreciated for, including her porcelain skin, her beauty and her dignity, to mark the fact that she belonged to one of the most important families in Florence, Leonardo still added his own personal style to the painting by giving Ginevra the personality, the strength and the tridimensionality that was always lacking from other painters' works of art of the time. That is probably why Leonardo was a perfect interpreter of the Renaissance period, as he perfectly embodied a more advanced, pioneering time in Italy and the rest of Europe.

Leonardo had the kind of talent that could add a personality to his works; he would take a stand against flat characters, pale religious representations, he would add a quality, a characteristic and ultimately a strong narrative to his works, something so pure that it had a deep impact on visual art as we know it. It didn't matter what he set his mind on, Leonardo had the extraordinary ability to mutate, change and improve whatever he touched.

At the time, particularly during his apprenticeship with Verrocchio, many are the stories told and retold about Leonardo and his talents, many explored and mentioned by Vasari in his biography. At first, he became famous for making terracotta statues, which showed a gift and a talent which were unusual for someone who had not received a formal artistic education. The work was so beautiful that it left everyone shocked; it seemed that everything he touched would acquire a different level of beauty. A particular episode comes to mind as told by Vasari, which brings us to a time when Leonardo had first started sketching. Sketching was something incredibly important to Leonardo and he would do so sometimes even absentmindedly, sometimes to accompany his notes, sometimes to see on paper something he had only imagined in his head.

Vasari tells us the story of the famous drawing for Leonardo's friend Antonio Segni who was, at the time, master of the papal mint. The drawing, *Neptune and Sea Horses*, which is now unfortunately lost, was so realistic that it almost looked like Neptune himself could have jumped out of the frame, with his chariots, so perfectly reproduced, almost tridimensional. In his biography, Vasari mentioned that the drawing was donated by Fabio, Antonio's son, to Messer Giovanni Gaddi, a priest, with some powerful words as a dedication comparing Leonardo's Neptune to other representations of the sea god by Homer and Virgil.

The dedication was simple yet effective. If poets, geniuses, of the likes of Virgil and *The Odyssey*'s author Homer, managed to portray an image of Neptune in our head by only using their words, Leonardo, with his immeasurable talent, has finally given us something to see with our eyes, an image so deep and articulated that not even our minds, reading about Neptune and his stories by the greatest poets, could have ever possibly conjured it.

Leonardo is also described by Vasari as being an inconstant, almost unpredictable creature, a trait of his personality that definitely showed in his work or in the lack of it; he was famous for losing interest quickly, leaving works unfinished to the annoyance of his customers. He would often be almost aggressively assaulted by a new idea so that he would have to leave what he was working on behind and move on to a new project. Sometimes he would spend days not eating or drinking, just painting or working on his projects, then he would forget about them and come back to them later when he wanted, taking his time. Often, these brilliant ideas never turned into finished projects, but many argue that maybe that was exactly what he had meant for them in the first place; these projects were unfinished to us but may have been completed in his vision.

Another victim of Leonardo's lack of focus was the Medusa head, a panel which portrayed the sea monster with a hairdo of knotted snakes, which was also never finished.

Leonardo loved to try new things when it came to painting; he experimented with different techniques, including something related to adopting different levels of darkness and shades in his works, something he called 'the sfumato technique'. That is exactly why in some of his earliest paintings we can see some heads painted and portrayed as floating or even wandering in a sea of the deepest black as their background. This particular technique had the merit of exalting Leonardo's figures even more, as these were then painted with a much lighter touch of colour. Vasari noted that Leonardo was clearly playing with the idea of achieving perfection, particularly when it came to colours and the balance of light and dark in all his paintings.

In his notes and biography, Vasari also captured a Leonardo who was fascinated with people. Before Leonardo's obsession with the human body, how it operated and worked on its own so effortlessly, Vasari gives us a man who was mostly captivated by people, who they were, what they did, and was found to be particularly taken by those who shared a trait, something peculiar, something different to anyone else, something that would have made them who they were.

Vasari noted that Leonardo would follow people around all day, particularly so if they showed any unusual facial trait that really stood out: an untamed beard, an important nose, something that would disrupt and grab Leonardo's attention. He would then memorise their expression, go home and paint them by heart.

At this stage in his career, many were the drawings he made of men and women; he did not only paint ordinary people but also some interesting personalities of the time, including Italian explorer Amerigo Vespucci in black chalk, and Scaramuccia, head of the gipsies. Even then, despite him painting well-known personalities and characters, he would still make sure to add some interesting touches to his paintings; that is the case in his version of Scaramuccia, who is portrayed from the back and whose drawing focuses on his rather grotesque head.

His fascination with people and his preferences for perfectly opposing black to light in his paintings can clearly be noticed in *The Adoration of the Magi*; in this painting it is interesting to note how several elements of Leonardo's techniques finally come together organically. This includes his fascination with people and people's expressions (in this painting, every person is different, every expression tells a story) and his partiality to the use of black to make his figures stand out. Once again, Leonardo's artistry and unreliable behaviour stopped him from finishing the painting, with *The Adoration of the Magi* remaining sadly another one of his unfinished works.

Chapter 3

Leonardo, the Lover

The Saltarelli affair

It is April 1476, the Renaissance is a prolific, happy period and homosexuality is the norm – not legal, but certainly widely accepted. In April 1476, someone, we will never know who, denounces a group of young men caught having sex. The notarised copy of the accusation leaves very little to the imagination.

In Florence, Leonardo is still working with Verrocchio while staying at his studio. He is a young painter who is yet to find himself. He doesn't know what he will do, he doesn't know if he will ever leave Verrocchio behind and start his own studio; he wants to, he really does, but hasn't quite found the courage yet.

The accusation shakes his world and is addressed to the officers of the Signoria, the Government of Florence.

It is a direct accusation and starts by talking about Jacopo Saltarelli, a man who does not boast of a great reputation in Florence. Jacopo is the brother of someone called Giovanni Saltarelli. Together they live in the goldsmith's shop in Vacchereccia, which is located just opposite Il Buco, a local inn. It is a story with echoes of poverty; neither brother is wealthy and they don't come from a family of means, they do what they can to make ends meet. The accusation is not going to help their already straitened circumstances.

The description goes as far as mentioning Jacopo's age – he is 17, and his appearance – he has a predilection for dressing in black. According to the notarised charge, Jacopo has a tendency to be involved in immoral and sinful activities. It is specified that for many years he has provided these sorts of services to many people and only a few are going to be named and charged with him. The word 'sodomised' is only mentioned at the end of the accusation, before going ahead and listing all the people involved. These people are:

- Bartolomeo di Pasquino, a goldsmith, who lives on the Vacchereccia
- Baccino the doublet-maker, who was living near Orsanmichele
- Leonardo Tornabuoni, better known as 'Il Teri', again, someone who liked to dress in black
- And finally, Leonardo da Vinci, who is the son of Ser Piero da Vinci, and who at the time lives with sculptor Andrea del Verrocchio.

It's a public accusation, something that has the power to shame all the people involved. The tone is detached, naturally accusatory and meant to discredit the reputation of every single man who has been caught in the act. Saltarelli is defined as someone who habitually finds himself in these sorts of situations; he has been involved in similar circumstances several times, he is nothing short of a well-known prostitute who provides these kinds of services to the young men in the area. Everyone else lives nearby, or perhaps just works not far from Il Buco. The only two people worth mentioning, whose reputation could really be discredited, are Leonardo, who belongs to the da Vinci family – his father Ser Piero is even mentioned in the accusation – and Leonardo Tornabuoni, who is a member of the aristocratic Tornabuoni family and related to Lucrezia Tornabuoni, mother of Lorenzo the Magnificent.

This is the first time we have proof of Leonardo's homosexuality. Early biographers of Leonardo are vague when it comes to his sexuality. The only one who directly addresses the rumours is Giovanni Paolo Lomazzo, who imagines a conversation between Leonardo and Phidias, a great sculptor from classical antiquity where the two, perhaps for the first time, talk freely about Leonardo's homosexuality and his relationship with Giacomo Capriotti, his student, known by everyone else as Salai.

Even Vasari was incredibly vague when it came to Leonardo's homosexuality; the only thing he mentioned was Salai's beauty and how much Leonardo loved his curly hair.

Jacopo Saltarelli was, according to the charge, a young boy who probably grew up in Santa Croce, where Leonardo lived and worked. He was not there on his own that night, he was accused of having sex with four more men who mostly came from poor families, except for Lorenzo Tornabuoni.

Tornabuoni was highly sought after in Florence because of his family's connections and he represented the reason, perhaps the only reason, why the affair was quickly dismissed by the government; no one had further charges pressed and no one was threatened with imprisonment.

Despite the almost total absence of consequences, the whole experience had a deep impact on Leonardo and later, in his notes, he talked about the creation of different machines that would or could free men from prisons.

One thing is certain: the Saltarelli affair deeply influenced Leonardo and his world. It was not just something that touched him in his early life but rather something that had a profound impact on everything else from his career to his relationships and his own incapacity to express emotions. It would not be wrong to say that following the affair, and the public humiliation, Leonardo was never quite the same.

According to many historians and biographers, the Saltarelli affair was the reason or one of the reasons why Leonardo changed his attitude towards love, masculinity and even sex.

Many believe that he was probably embarrassed by what had happened; he was, after all, living with Verrocchio at the time, not quite independent yet, and coming from a Catholic education which must have had some influence and effect on his general upbringing. With his sexuality being broadcast for all Florence to see and judge, despite how open-minded the Renaissance had made Florentine people, he decided to take a step back and ignore the most human aspect of himself. It is right there, at that precise moment, that he started to develop a further detachment when it came to sex, let alone love; many biographers even swear that he was celibate for his entire life and that, despite being attracted to men, he did not get involved in further relationships.

Despite this, many others believe that Leonardo was far from being celibate and that he went on to have relationships with some of his students. He still never talked much about love, both from his personal point of view and from a more general perspective; he tended to avoid anything that was personal or that could touch him in any way. Therefore, for years, we have had to peruse his notes, having a look at his work, searching for his interpretation of love in his paintings, in his work and in his quotes.

'Life without love is no life at all,' he used to say. It would be interesting to understand whether he thought he had loved in his life or not; whether, in this quote, he had intended to talk about romantic love or otherwise.

With his name being attached to all sorts of things, it is rare to find the master and the genius, Leonardo himself, vocalising his thoughts when it came to love – if by love we mean a form of romantic love, rather than anything that was more universal and involved the love and the admiration he felt for the world and its beauties, including nature.

Of course, it is probable that Leonardo was not talking about love in the most romantic sense, let alone sexual, as he was a lifelong student who would always show, until the end of his days, a strong love for anything that was new and unknown to him. Learning was probably the most well known and confirmed lover of his life. His mind was too quick, his attention span too short to focus on anything but his insatiable thirst and love for knowledge. Yet he did have lovers, famous ones, people he cared about and who represented for him an anchor, maybe the only one, capable of keeping him grounded in the present.

Being an artist, always busying himself with the most interesting personalities of the time, offering his artistry to the most influential patrons and providing the world with his most beautiful works yet, it is interesting to reflect on the fact that, before any of this, Leonardo was a man, and much like any other man he was rumoured to be entangled in several relationships, often long-term, with different people who would populate his fascinating and mysterious universe.

As confirmed by several other biographers and researchers, Leonardo was homosexual at a time when homosexuality was not allowed and where sodomy was a *reato*, a crime. Especially in Italy, and particularly in Florence, in 1432, the government established a committee meant to tackle the sodomy issue and created what was then called the Office of the Night, with members required to investigate charges of sodomy.

Despite this, and granted how contradictory these times were, Florence remained a liberal, artistic city during the Renaissance and it is reported by several researchers that many members of the Office of the Night used to cover up and quickly dismiss actions against those accused of sodomy, including Leonardo. They were well known for turning a blind eye to homosexual people as Florence boasted an extraordinarily open mind for the time.

Many believe that the heart of the Renaissance's gay scene was Ponte Vecchio, a medieval bridge which represented a pivotal centre for homosexual people, who used to work in nearby shops, with its inn, Il Buco (which translates in English as 'The Hole').

According to author Michael Rocke, author of *Forbidden Friendships: Homosexuality and Male Friendship in Renaissance Florence*, Ponte Vecchio acted as a meeting place for homosexual men during the Renaissance time.

According to Rocke, at the time about 17,000 people were accused of sodomy, and according to his findings, these men were not all homosexual but considered sodomy part of the open-minded, liberal Florentine culture of the time. Of course, some, if not most of them, were homosexuals and ended up having several relationships with men despite being in long-term relationships with women or even being married.

Many men would also marry each other and make it official, with the Office of the Night sometimes regarding these unions as official marriages. Often, homosexual relationships were even accepted by the rest of the family, especially if they could lead to some level of progress and advancement in careers; older lovers represented an easy way to ensure a prosperous future from a financial point of view for the individual and even his relatives. In his book, Rocke found that despite the big number of people accused of sodomy, not everyone was convicted, with numbers showing less than 3,000 people being convicted, and with the rest of them never even paying a fine. Leonardo, who was accused of sodomy not once but twice, was never convicted; many have speculated about the fact that in both cases he was accused of sodomy while being in the company of two young men who belonged to important, sought-after families of the time. Also, many researchers argue that the Office of the Night never had the intention of incriminating anyone until forced to do so by the government and that sodomy, despite being illegal, was very much allowed during Renaissance times and the Florence of the time. It worked as a silent agreement, something that had been in place since the very beginning when the Office of the Night had been established and that kept going until its dissolution.

Homosexual relationships were tolerated and accepted by everyone else involved – family, friends, relatives – and it was not unusual for the couple to spend time together, attend events, go to the pub, embrace

Florence's vibrant culture of gambling, or why not go on a trip together to their house in the country? It was out in the open, yet it was not legal, and many people took the matter into their own hands to lift the homosexuality ban; in the town of Prato, for example, a box intended to store sodomy accusations was taken down. Much later, in 1512, a group of young men from a family of means started one of the first gay rights demonstrations in history, demanding that sodomy sentences be revoked.

Following the Saltarelli case, many believe that Leonardo had given up on the idea of love or being in love with someone; feelings were not something he succeeded in expressing clearly unless it was through the medium of his works, his paintings, his inventions, and not something that made him comfortable or in control, and when it came to love he was no different.

He did not leave many works, notebooks or words about love. He knew it was important, he had seen its power, and he was no stranger to its beauty, yet despite being able to convey its message in his works, if you see all the beautiful portraits he had created for men in love, like the one of Ginevra de Benci, or perhaps even the *Mona Lisa*, he was never quite able to express love in his notebooks. He was much more taken by the body and how it worked so perfectly.

Leonardo always seemed shy when it came to sharing his feelings, and his notebooks are proof of that. He was not prepared to talk about love – he never was; it was something to do with the culture of the time, men did not express their feelings as such unless they were in a committed relationship but, even then, it was a proof of virility rather than emotionally driven.

For a man who managed to maintain such discretion when it came to love, it comes as a surprise then that Leonardo had not only one but two important men who could be defined today as the biggest loves of his life, the ones he left everything to, and perhaps the ones he loved the most.

Leonardo and Salai

He is not dressed for a formal event, he is not elegant or composed. You can tell he is very young, perhaps 12 or 14. He is in fancy dress, posing with the strength of his youth, a strength that says, 'here I am'. Fearless, challenging the world, or anything that could be new and scary, conscious of his power, of his role, a role that would make him an important, if not a fundamental, element in the life of the person creating his portrait. He almost reminds everyone of a young David, in Verrocchio's masterpiece statue; he is arrogant, confident, almost cocky of his master's affection. He is, after all, a little devil, or a Salai.

The first man in Leonardo's life, the one who probably inspired him the most was Salai, his pupil, his friend and then, his lover. Salai, which means 'little devil' or 'the unclean one', was the name Leonardo himself attributed to him. Born in 1480, he was named Gian Giacomo Caprotti da Oreno and, throughout his life, he played a strong part in Leonardo's.

Salai was the son of Pietro di Giovanni, who served as the tenant of Leonardo's vineyard in Milan. He joined Leonardo's household at the age of 10 and stayed with his master, becoming then his alleged lover for as many as thirty years, and being with Leonardo almost up until his death.

In one of his most famous quotes, Leonardo talks about Salai depicting an accurate portrait of his favourite pupil. He calls Salai a thief, a glutton, stubborn, someone who would steal from him on a regular basis. That is how Leonardo gave him the nickname of a little devil, Salai. It is reported that he stole from Leonardo several times, something Leonardo always forgave him for.

Leonardo and Salai had a very strong relationship and Salai would often accompany Leonardo on his trips. They most certainly inspired each other for a lifetime; Leonardo loved having him around and Salai was incredibly good with the financial aspect of their little family business; in several letters, Leonardo mentions Salai when writing to his patrons as someone who would go to discuss matters related to compensation.

Researchers also found several erotic sketches of Salai which would prove their romantic relationship. These include *Angel Incarnate* which is a prior sketch of the John the Baptist painting (Salai served as a model for this painting), which shows Salai with an erection.

Salai did not just work as a model for Leonardo but he was a student and studied art; he was a decent painter himself but never succeeded in becoming as famous as his master.

In many ways, Salai remained the little devil in fancy dress in Leonardo's portrait for most of his life. He didn't know, could not know any other way to be – he was dearly loved by Leonardo, always at his master's side, and he is also the one accused of selling most of Leonardo's works following his death, including the *Mona Lisa*. He even died like the little devil that he had been his entire life, following his marriage to a woman, Bianca Coldirodi d'Annono. Salai died in 1524 at the age of 43, after being wounded during a duel.

Leonardo and Francesco Melzi

Not many people understood Leonardo like Francesco Melzi, not even Salai. Francesco was another important character populating Leonardo's universe. He was shyer, a bit more reserved than Salai, yet he became invaluable to Leonardo and was one of the few who stayed with him until the very end.

Francesco Melzi was born in 1490 and, according to Vasari, he was an eclectic and highly mysterious character in Leonardo's universe. He was from Milan, a nobleman belonging to a family of means who started training at Leonardo's studio in the city when he was quite young. His skills as a painter were not often understood or appreciated but, compared to other students and artists who used to work at Leonardo's, Melzi's talent was not as distinguishable.

One of Melzi's best works was *The Flora*, which had some similarities with other works of Leonardo, particularly resembling his style when it came to the sfumato and the use of androgynous figures. In *The Flora*, Melzi also succeeded in establishing, much like his master, a strong narrative between characters. According to classical mythology, Flora was the wife of Zephyr, the west wind of springtime; she was the mother of all the plants, the one who brings life, and in Melzi's work she is portrayed with naked breasts, emerging from a mysterious grotto covered with various flowers, while she is gracefully looking at a blue flower which symbolises fertility.

The Flora still stands today as Melzi's most important painting, reminding us of Leonardo and his style in so many ways; not only from the sfumato perspective but also from nature, love and a passion for the botanical sciences, something he shared with his master.

Melzi had much more in common with Leonardo compared to Salai, particularly in terms of sensitivity and talent; the two shared a love for the arts as well as for science; for example, the body of *The Flora* follows the same human body principles found in Leonardo's research.

Following Leonardo's death, Melzi inherited most of Leonardo's collection, which included different works of art, books, instruments and most importantly his notebooks, the Codices.

Many biographers and researchers believe him to be one of Leonardo's best pupils and lover, and, despite Salai's jealousy, he was soon accepted and became part of Leonardo's world, taking different trips with his master.

Born from a noble family in Milan, Melzi was incredibly highly regarded by Leonardo for his charisma and style of painting. He joined Leonardo's workshop in Milan in 1508, and became part of the loyal group of friends and lovers who ended up following him around from Milan to Rome and then even to France, where he stayed until Leonardo passed away in 1519.

Leonardo and the Renaissance idea of love

Although Leonardo was never interested in love, or never really talked about love in the romantic sense, love was an important chapter of the Renaissance era.

At the time, it was common for couples to have a platonic relationship and for courtship to go through different stages which included gift exchanges often involving beautiful, bespoke portraits of the object of affection; it was the norm for men to admire their women from afar, producing a vast array of platonic demonstrations of love from poems to painting or music.

During the Italian Renaissance, couples could not consummate their love during courtship so they preferred to exchange gifts instead; usually, these objects embodied symbolic representations – it was common to present the beloved one with representations of the phoenix, the legendary bird that burns but resurrects from its ashes.

Some men were also more creative and wrote songs in order to pivot the attention of their lover their way. One thing was certain: during the Renaissance, people had a different way to see love and marriage. If the first was something poets talked about, for example, the nostalgia of love itself was enough for some artists to create some highly creative representations in the arts and through different media forms (it was a strong force, a union of souls and bodies, something which was both spiritual and sexual), the latter was a much more practical affair, something families availed themselves of in order to create alliances and was hardly ever dictated by love. That is also why many people used to have a mistress on the side.

However, despite the matter of love and marriage being in contrast, it is interesting to note that during the Renaissance the concept of romantic love finally started to take shape, particularly related to the idea of courtship. The beloved, the lover, started to assume some perfect characteristics, particularly thanks to some Italian writers who became famous during the Renaissance including Dante Alighieri (who wrote about Beatrice) and Petrarch (who was consumed by his love for his Laura). Every poet had an impossible love, someone they could only dream of, someone unachievable for beauty, social position and someone who also had to remain unattainable to keep on generating more and more prose. Poets were different and some would also see love as sexual desire, while others were happy to take a higher perspective, connecting the idea of love with something not only pure and perfect but also ideal.

When it comes to love, many Renaissance creative men and artists saw platonic love as being one of the highest and noblest forms of love; this concept was developed and based on the ideas of the Neoplatonists who equally based their thoughts on Plato and then went on to define love as being a journey towards the divine. According to Plato, far from being attached to the idea of physical love, the concept of love is something to be connected to a more general ideal: at first, we are attracted to a beautiful individual, then to beautiful people in general, consequently to beautiful minds, ideas and then beauty itself.

Leonardo was never that spiritual when it came to love, as he was quite detached from the concept itself. Yet, being an artist, he became a favourite when it came to portrait paintings of some of the most sought-after women of the time.

Another trend during the Renaissance was the idea of love perpetuated by pastoral poetry, which kept a focus on shepherds and nymphs. For these poets, the countryside represented a perfect setting for the expression of honest feelings and simple pleasures. Despite this, love was not always perfect and ideal, and during the Renaissance an equally common trend was 'bawdy', which focused on simple crude sexuality and on women, who would be often portrayed as temptresses.

During the Renaissance, it was common to believe that everyday marriage had nothing to do with love; marriage was based on money, social status and convenience. However, despite this, there were many people who decided to go against family and marry for love; these cases were quite rare as the feelings of the couple were rarely taken into consideration. It was far more important to build alliances based on finance and family politics. Marriage contracts were also often the norm; arranged marriages were not only something for wealthy families but also between couples from a lower social level. However, despite this, couples coming from the lower classes had more freedom and had more contact with their beloved, often far away from their families' eyes, sometimes on a daily basis.

Differences applied when it came to the concept of being betrothed as this represented an intermediate step between courtship and marriage and could only be broken if both parties agreed. Being betrothed to someone was a promise, sometimes a pledge, which was taken with a priest; often women complained that men would only be betrothed so that they could have sex with them and then leave them behind, failing to fulfil their promise and cement the betrothal with marriage. Courtship was quickly abandoned after marriage, as marriage had nothing to do with passion and often men would find that elsewhere with their mistress or mistresses, fathering children outside marriage.

But where did Leonardo find his place when it came to love and courtship, let alone marriage? We know that he never married, not even for convenience or because society demanded him to, and we don't know if that lost him any work or any favours with some of the princes of the time. He was homosexual and had several lovers, yet he doesn't seem to have been close to any women, not even as a friend.

Leonardo had the chance to work with different women for several patrons and, by doing so, he had the opportunity to learn about them, often adding details to their portraits that would make them stand out, and which would make them more than just an object of desire. These women had a story, a personality and something that went above and beyond, something Leonardo was able to recognise. It is interesting to note the fundamental impact Leonardo had on women during the

Renaissance, succeeding in altering the way they were perceived by the society of the time a little.

During the Renaissance, women didn't have much choice; they were not left with many options when it came to their future or their life. Despite this, many researchers have strongly argued that women, especially those belonging to the wealthiest families, boasted much more independence than those from previous eras; but still they had to conform to patriarchal society rules which wanted them to marry and be defined by marriage.

This thesis has often been opposed by researchers, including Joan Kelly Gadol, who in her article 'Did women have a Renaissance?' concludes that, in fact, they did not. In her essay, she writes that despite Italy flourishing during the Renaissance from both an economic and cultural point of view, it failed to drag women into a similar revolution. In particular, when it comes to noblewomen, she argues that their role was reduced to an aesthetic object, as they remained chaste or often dependent on their husbands. However, despite what Gadol argues, many researchers believe that during the Renaissance women boasted a much more interesting social position; they seemed to conquer a role which saw them acting as powerful patrons of artists and also becoming artists themselves, especially in Florence where women of the time could participate and be more actively involved in the life of the city.

Although, much like Gadol, many other researchers confirm that despite the beauty and the artistic advancement of such a positive period, women still maintained a less important position within the society of the time, something that economic progress and cultural improvements could do nothing about.

To start with, women maintained a tendency to get married quite young, often while they were still in their teens. They rarely married their peers but tended to accept the courtship of and consequently marry older men. They would often be put in charge of family life, of the house, of the children, and they would often take a more domestic role. When left widowed by their already elderly husbands, they would be urged to get married again soon. Outside family life and the education of their children, they did not have other worries or interests, let alone much control over their own life. Having a family was their only guarantee of a position within society; if celibate or widowed they would often be forced to become nuns even without a true vocation and live off their craftwork within the nunnery.

Often, women from the middle classes became tradeswomen and helped their husbands or fathers in their shop, starting to establish and benefit from a certain level of power and control over their life. According to several researchers, often middle-class women would succeed in having more independence and freedom; despite still working with their husbands, they would still hold an important position as part of the society of the time. Fascinated as he was by the female universe, Leonardo's representation of women remains different from anything we have ever witnessed in the history of art; his women are perfect and angelic yet never completely flawless – attractive, yes, but with a little something extra no one can quite fully grasp. Leonardo has the merit of portraying women as they are by equally successfully adding little details that confirm their inner rebellion; behind their perfect traits Leonardo's female figures appear to be in power. They are often accused of being cold and detached like the Virgin Mary in *The Annunciation* or, later on, flirtatious and mysterious like the *Mona Lisa*. Leonardo adds an extra layer of personality to his female subjects, creating female figures which contradistinguish themselves for their depth, wisdom and personality. In many ways, Leonardo had the intelligence to include women's personalities in his paintings. It did not matter if they were biblical characters or women of means, he took them and added an extra layer to his portrait painting. Leonardo's women are not just there to be looked at by their beloved; they are there because there is something that has not been quite revealed about them, they are not only asking to be admired but also, and most importantly, to be understood. Love is something they attract but there is also something else about them, a smile that hides a secret, a rebel curl in their hair, something that is not quite as perfect as the world would like them to be. Leonardo knows that by painting them, representing them, in a more imperfect manner, he will manage to finally show the world that there is so much more than love, marriage and beauty when it comes to Renaissance women.

Chapter 4

Leonardo and the Medici

Leonardo worked at Verrocchio's studio for a very long time, even after qualifying as a master in the Guild of Saint Luke, an association of artists, and setting up his own workshop. Perhaps he just couldn't bear to be far away from his master, or perhaps, in many ways, he felt and acted like an eternal student.

He left Verrocchio's studio in 1478 with a commission of his own. Fully confident of his own talent and capabilities, the boy who had served as a model for Verrocchio's David had finally grown up. He was not that little lad, full of arrogance, anymore; he was a man, a talented man who was going to change the world by being a passionate inventor, philosopher and, of course, an acclaimed painter.

Leaving Verrocchio, his master, behind must not have been easy but Leonardo was already an artist in his own right, and he was willing to explore and learn as much as he could about the world and himself.

At first, he was commissioned to paint an altarpiece for the Chapel of St Bernard at the Palazzo Vecchio, a work he did not finish; instead he let artist Filippino Lippi continue for him. Lippi successfully based his work on Leonardo's outline, establishing then a series of angelic figures and saints with the Virgin Mary; the figures of the angels remind us of those of both Verrocchio and Leonardo.

In 1480, Leonardo started a new phase in his life, a phase that influenced his entire artistic career, something that finally cemented his position as an independent artist and then a genius: he started to work with the Medici family, one of the most important Italian families and Florence's rulers.

As part of his work for the Medici and under their patronage, Leonardo often worked from a garden in Piazza San Marco in Florence where other protégés of the Medici used to paint, create and talk about art. It was an interesting, eclectic and highly motivational moment in

Leonardo's and in these artists' lives; they would compete with each other, yet thrive off each other too. Patronage represented security and easy money for the artists of the time as it gave them the chance to grow as professional artists and build long-lasting relationships with families of means.

The system of patronage was not as straightforward as many would think. According to Peter Burke's *The Italian Renaissance: Culture and Society in Italy*, there were up to five different systems of patronage that could be established between artists and patrons (those who would benefit from the services offered by artists) at the time, with some of these systems still present today.

The first one is the classic and, perhaps, the most diffused in Italy, the one even Leonardo was under during his time working for the Medici family during the Renaissance. This system of patronage was called the household system and involved the presence of a rich man or family hosting the artist in their house, offering board, lodging and even gifts from time to time, in exchange for having a constant selection of creative works produced by the artist whenever the patron wanted.

The second system was based on commission. Still founded on a strong relationship between the creative person and the patron, this system was more temporary than the first one and it usually lasted until the work was delivered.

The third system was called, and still is today, the market system, whereby the artist produced something he felt was of value enough to be showcased in a market environment and usually sold it to patrons or customers on an ad hoc basis.

According to Burke, there were also different patron categories, which included people working in the church system, and that would explain the copious number of religious paintings, and those working for the government; it was, after all, the Government of Florence, the Signoria, which, for example, commissioned Leonardo's unfinished and mysterious painting of *The Battle of Anghiari*.

The most obvious difference between being taken on board by a patron compared to just having a temporary relationship dependent on the delivery of the work was that the first entailed financial security and a higher position in society. Despite this, at the death of a patron, many were the artists who found themselves without anything to fall back on. One of these was Vasari, who was working for the Duke of

Florence, Alessandro de' Medici. After the murder of the duke, Vasari found himself with nothing and in the uncomfortable, difficult position of having to find another patron. Something which he eventually did when he entered the service of Cosimo, the successor of Alessandro.

But what was the motivation behind art patronage? According to Burke, there were four: piety, prestige, pleasure and, potentially, investment; often piety and compassionate reasons were mentioned in contracts. Prestige was one of the most popular motivations, as it was important to show the world that the family in question had reached an important position in society; often this had political implications, with patronage helping a family to emerge in the political culture of the time. It was also common to become patrons of artists for pleasure as a way of expressing a certain partiality and passion for the arts. The relationship between an artist and his patron was not always perfect, and often they would get into conflict over money; wealthy patrons would pay artists' debts but would also become demanding and overwhelming in their requests. Often, artists would be unhappy with the commissioned work as they did not feel it expressed their artistry fully, and often patrons would not be happy about the final work produced and threaten to cut artists off.

An interesting story regarding the relationship between an artist and a patron is told once again by Giorgio Vasari when he talks about painter Piero di Cosimo, who was commissioned to paint a picture for the Foundling Hospital in Florence but refused to show the picture before it was finished to his patron, the director of the hospital. The conflict saw the director threatening not to pay Piero for his work and Piero threatening, from his side, to destroy the painting.

An influential family who ruled Florence during the Renaissance, the Medici were Leonardo's first patrons. At first, they were fascinated by Leonardo and his work; they were taken by eclectic, unique people who could bring something different to their court and enrich their incredible collection of painters, artists, writers and generally creative people. However, they quickly lost interest. There are several theories which could explain the Medici relationship with Leonardo. Several researchers have speculated that Leonardo, in being so unpredictable in his ways, in his own methodology of working, leaving several projects unfinished, could have been judged as being not reliable, as not being as focused as other painters or artists of the time who populated the Medici court.

Other theories argue that Leonardo's homosexuality and his two sodomy accusations had been a step too far for one of the most important families in Italy; perhaps they didn't want to associate their name with Leonardo's and lose their reputation while doing so. However, that is a weak theory; according to many researchers, during the Renaissance homosexuality was not legal but still widely accepted.

Despite their imperfect relationship, both Leonardo and the Medici worked together and fed off each other's passion for the arts. Originally from a little village in Tuscany called Cafaggiolo, the Medici family emigrated to Florence around the twelfth century and distinguished themselves for their love and appreciation of the arts, becoming patrons of several sought-after artists of their time; they ruled Florence twice and for a very long time, losing influence following the city being proclaimed a republic but coming back to power shortly after; the new republic was un-proclaimed and Pope Clement VII appointed Alessandro de' Medici as Duke of the Florentine Republic.

The family found its origins in Giovanni di Bicci de' Medici. He was the one who started the arts patronage for which the family grew famous; Giovanni commissioned new bronze doors for the baptistry in Florence, a commission won by artist Lorenzo Ghiberti, who took a lifetime (over forty years) to finish the work. The doors were so beautiful that even Michelangelo Buonarroti could not help but call them Gates to Paradise. The Gates to Paradise were nothing other than panels framed by two strips on the sides, made of bronze, and adorned with beautiful biblical characters and prophets and twenty-four more heads of different prophets and sibyls.

If the strips had a religious theme with prophets and scenes from the Bible, the architraves showed a more natural theme, featuring different elements including plants and animals. Ghiberti's style was strongly influenced by another famous artist of the time, Donatello. Working on those panels for over forty years, Ghiberti focused on one particular topic, the 'salvation', with panels illustrating sin and representing the role of God and the coming of Christ. Other panels narratively and structurally developed later by Ghiberti, including the Isaac one, featured a combination of different figures and landscapes as well as quotes.

It is in this world of strong artistic inspiration that Leonardo moved and learnt from the best, inspired by the wealthiest family in Florence, a family that was determined to make the arts the essence of the Renaissance.

Giovanni's son Cosimo ruled Florence until his death and, much like his father, he started taking an interest in the arts, succeeding in turning Florence into the Renaissance's capital of culture due to his incredible artists and works of art. Cosimo was mostly known as Cosimo the Elder and boasted a reputation for being an art patron and general art lover, devoted to his artists who included Brunelleschi, Ghiberti, of course, and Donatello, who under his patronage created *David*. According to Bard Thompson's *Humanists and Reformers*, Cosimo was a complex man who had received a Christian education and was both a politician and a businessman; very soon, he decided not to show off his power, preferring to ride a mule rather than a horse. He also refused Brunelleschi's architectural plans for a luxury Medici palace, as he was not a fan of anything that was opulent and too ostentatious, preferring to maintain a simple, subtle presence in Florence.

Despite this, he did all that was in his power in the name of the arts, investing as much as he could in improving Florence from an artistic point of view: Cosimo was an acclaimed patron, and under his patronage the Dominican convent of San Marco was reconstructed by architect Michelozzo. According to Thompson, Cosimo spent about 7 million florins on the building, with work taking more than thirty years: the convent was also the perfect place to store Cosimo's incredible collection of books, as well as his protégé humanist de Niccoli's volumes. After dismissing Brunelleschi and his extravagances, Cosimo even asked Michelozzo to work on the Medici palace, going for a more simple decor.

Cosimo was an extraordinary patron and he was able to work with some of the most interesting artists of the time; this included Donatello, one of his favourite artists, and several others, including Fra Filippo Lippi, a friar who had not exactly fully committed to the religious life and was intimate with many women. Lippi even became a father after having a relationship with a nun, a model he had chosen for his Madonna for an altarpiece, and in order to help him and give him some direction in life, Cosimo decided to lock him in the Medici Palace. Despite Cosimo's efforts, Lippi succeeded in escaping and continued his debauched lifestyle.

Cosimo's grandson, Lorenzo the Magnificent (Il Magnifico), sealed Florence's status as one of the most important cultural centres of the Renaissance's arts and humanities, not only in Italy but also in Europe. His career was tainted by two important events. The first occurred during the revolt of Volterra, where he employed Federico da Montefeltro, Duke of Urbino, to end protests against his ruling. The duke proved unable to control the troops who ravaged the city, leaving Lorenzo to take the blame. The second event was the Pazzi Conspiracy, a coup d'état which aimed to unseat the Medici family from Florence and ended with the murder of Lorenzo's brother, Giuliano.

Lorenzo was a strong personality, ruthless, fearless, but also an artist, a writer and a poet; he adored surrounding himself with the most interesting personalities and artists of the time including Botticelli, Michelangelo and, of course, Leonardo. Lorenzo was often described as being a diplomat, a politician, and a patron, and following his brother Giuliano's murder he was the only ruler of Florence from 1478 to 1492. His father, Piero, was a capable, smart man who had perfectly combined politics with economic affairs; he was not only Florence's ruler but also the founder of the Medici Bank.

When it came to his predilection for the arts, it is believed that Lorenzo took after his mother Lucrezia, a writer and a friend of many artists and sought-after personalities in the cultural panorama of the Florence of the time. Lucrezia Tornabuoni was a woman like no other. She boasted influence over the politics and culture of Florence and often over her own son, Lorenzo. She belonged to two of the wealthiest families in Florence, the Tornabuoni and Guicciardini, and had married Piero, the eldest son of Cosimo de' Medici. She became the 'prima donna' (the first woman) of the city and it certainly helped that her family was so influential: she was sister to Giovanni Tornabuoni, a banker; wife of Piero de' Medici, the head of the Republic; mother of Lorenzo 'the Magnificent'; and grandmother of Leo X and Clement VII, future popes. She was very much loved not only by the people in Florence but also and especially by her son Lorenzo, who after her death said he hadn't only lost a mother, but also his only refuge.

Lucrezia was very present in the life of her family and acted as a confidante and wise adviser to most people. She was not a typical noblewoman housewife of the Renaissance; she was a businesswoman, a patron, a political diplomat and an artist in her own right with a predilection for poetry. Her writings were of religious nature but she was also interested in trade and war affairs. Lucrezia also took care of collecting rents on the properties she owned in Pisa, took charge of the remodelling work on thermal baths, and made sure to run the day-to-day activities of the family when her husband, who was often sick, couldn't. Lucrezia was also a highly charitable person, who managed a charity for poor girls.

According to Thompson, Lucrezia went to Rome to properly inspect Clarice Orsini, who belonged to one of the most important families in Rome and was intended to become Lorenzo's bride. Clarice had an interesting story of her own: born in 1453, she received a Catholic education and moved to Florence after marrying Lorenzo. Clarice was perfect; she was modest yet came from a wealthy, well-known family. She also didn't like to be in the spotlight, something that Lorenzo, a slightly narcissistic personality, often craved. Her marriage to Lorenzo was not a happy one. Clarice came from a strong Catholic upbringing, something that didn't correspond to Florence and its artistic ways. She and Lorenzo were not on the same page on several things, including the education of their ten children, who all received a traditional Catholic upbringing.

From the very beginning, when only a child, Lorenzo proved himself to be a very astute and intelligent boy, something that granted him the attribute of 'the Magnificent' everywhere he went. Because of his attitude towards the arts and humanities, Lorenzo was taught by the best teachers of his time and attended the Platonic Academy (Accademia Platonica), which was a group of students who would meet to discuss philosophy and the classics under the guidance of philosopher Marsilio Ficino. While spending time at the academy, Lorenzo also learnt to play the lyre and sing while also further exploring his love for poetry and the arts. No wonder he became close to artists like Leonardo and craved their presence at his court.

He had many artists at his court and was an important patron to them all, yet he did not often commission them, and when Leonardo decided to leave and embark on his new adventure in Milan, he was not too sad to lose his talent and work.

Leonardo was not his favourite artist, whereas Antonio del Pollaiuolo, a painter, sculptor and goldsmith, came pretty close. Lorenzo also worked with Michelangelo, who had been recommended to him by Ghirlandaio himself as one of his most promising students.

Something remarkable about Lorenzo and the way he interpreted patronage was the learning focus he gave to it: particularly so when it came to universities, as he went on to improve both the University of

Pisa and the University of Florence, making the latter a centre for the learning of classical Greek.

A charmer and an overall fascinating character, Lorenzo entered politics very young and started a range of reforms which did not only have a positive impact on institutions, bringing to a halt all existing rivalries between families of means and power in Florence, but also contributed to bringing a period of peace among the different Italian rulers of the time thanks to his diplomacy skills, which granted him the favour of many political and religious personalities including the Pope.

Researchers and historians have a tendency to condemn Lorenzo, despite appreciating his role being pivotal during the Renaissance, as they believe him to be a despot and, often, define him as being nothing short of a dictator who left very little power to people as well as to municipal courts which had very little autonomy during his rule, with Lorenzo keeping everything close and largely in his hands. Despite this, it would be impossible not to acknowledge the fact that under his influence Florence went through a highly prolific cultural time during the Renaissance.

The Medici were pioneers in everything the Renaissance stood for and its members also supported Galileo Galilei financially in his scientific discoveries (despite taking a step back so as not to taint their reputation when Galilei's discoveries became too heretic for the time), which ultimately led him to challenge and question everything he had been taught and finally discover that the Earth orbits the Sun rather than the opposite.

It is understandable that an artistic soul like Lorenzo the Magnificent could be captivated by artists, including someone like Leonardo. Leonardo was a sensitive, positive, almost luminous creature; he was the artist and the master, the painter who did not only paint but also, in every sense of the word, created a whole universe of artistic possibilities with his work.

Lorenzo was the one who understood, celebrated and enabled the arts, one of the many artists who made Florence what it was: a city of beauty, talent and incredible artistic innovation and energy.

Under and for the Medici family, Leonardo worked on different projects which started both his career as an artist and his independence from Verrocchio, his first master. Far from working on his painting, Leonardo was commissioned to work on an altarpiece, something which did not turn out to be something of great interest to him. However, finally, in 1478, he was commissioned by the Medici family to work on *The Adoration of the Magi*, managing thus to obtain the seal of approval of the powerful Italian family and their academy's exclusive circle of artists, philosophers and writers, which was often defined as Neoplatonic as it originated from Platonic philosophy.

Much like most of his works, both the altarpiece for the Chapel of St Bernard in Florence's Palazzo Vecchio and *The Adoration of the Magi* remained unfinished, with no particular explanation to justify his sudden lack of interest.

That essentially brought Leonardo's relationship with the Medici family to an end. It almost looked like he felt he had not been given enough to stimulate him, to motivate him, and to inspire him. Leonardo was not an artist in that sense; he was much more interested in creating different solutions to city problems, he was starting to realise that perhaps a lifetime as a visual artist was not what he had envisioned for his career, not what he wanted to be remembered for.

He started to play with other ideas. It was the Renaissance, and men could be whoever they wanted to be, and there were so many different professions he could do instead: he was an inventor, he had a mathematical mind, he was interested in medicine, and he could just come up with theories and ideas that could perhaps be of more use to patrons, definitely more practical than just another painting.

It was this sudden realisation that led Leonardo to finally leave Florence, Tuscany and the Medici family and lay the foundations for a different adventure, something that eventually would bring him to the court of another powerful man, Ludovico Sforza.

Chapter 5

Leonardo, the Renaissance Genius

The room quietens. You can feel the anticipation when the lights go off and the show comes to life, it's the moon, coming down from the sky, and men dressed as angels, and do we see planets? It's the Renaissance as we have never seen it before, it's the Renaissance taking shape and form in light and colours, shades we didn't even know could exist. There are gods, no matter what sort of gods, you can feel their supremacy, their power, descending from their world, coming to the Earth to come to talk to us; their words are kind, they are talking about a particular beauty in the room. It's her, this is all for her: the bride; these gods talk about her virtues, her qualities, the wonderful Renaissance attributes a woman of her position must necessarily possess and then, naturally, the music starts, because we would not have expected anything else: it is a musical, after all, yet it is still a party, it's 'the party of paradise'.

The party of paradise was an event, a party, a gathering and a theatre piece all in one, something Leonardo personally created, developed and directed to mark a wonderful one-of-a-kind occasion: the wedding of Gian Galeazzo Maria Sforza and Isabella d'Aragona, during his time under the patronage of the Sforza family.

For the party of paradise, Leonardo had the wit and the ability to wear different artistic hats for the production of the event; these included art director, scriptwriter and engineer. The party of paradise was an event which is still talked of today, still praised and still brought as an example of Leonardo's talent. The party took place in the 'Sala Verde' in the Sforza's Castle and, according to the testimonials of those who had the chance to attend such an exclusive event, it was a moment of joy, beauty and talent that did not only define Leonardo, freezing him in his position as maestro and genius, but also the Renaissance as a pioneering period for the love of the arts and for experimentation with new techniques.

When it came to Leonardo, no better event marked Leonardo's genius and creativity, yet there are no official records of the party except for the testimonials of the people of the time and some sketches found in Leonardo's notebooks.

Leonardo was a creative man; he could do anything he wanted when it came to the arts, from event organising to painting the most exquisite works of art. He was also the perfect person to have at court, as he was a man full of life, who perfectly embodied the Renaissance and its beauties. He was also funny and interesting and interested in everyone and everything. He was a beautiful man with long hair, perhaps blonde, or more like strawberry blonde; a lighter, blonder shade of red, as many believe. He also had beautiful blue eyes, so magnetic that people could hardly look elsewhere. He was extravagant, yet handsome, and he could fill the room with his personality and his charisma.

He was partial to fashion and to short dresses and colourful tights, he had a strong charisma and there was really nothing he couldn't do. He had a beautiful voice, and many people from his time remember him singing and maybe improvising with his favourite instrument, the lira da braccio. He was such a good singer and musician that he even wrote a song, adding musician and lyricist to the many things he could do.

The lyrics of the song are emotional and touching and maybe show us a Leonardo who is a little different to the man we have been told about. We remember the detached scientist but don't always get to see the human being, someone who had such a delicate, sweet nature that was capable of composing the most heart-breaking music.

The song he wrote has some passionate lyrics which say 'Quando l'amante è giunto all'amato si riposa', which loosely translate as 'When the lover comes back to the loved one, that's when he can rest'. We will never know who the song was for, who he had written such nostalgic words for, and we may wonder if these lyrics represent the key to understanding who the real Leonardo was.

One thing is certain: Leonardo was a brilliant man who was capable of expressing his thoughts and irony and sarcasm in his writing, in his work, in his fables and in the numerous notebooks which have been saved for us all to read and appreciate.

We can imagine him at court, any court, surrounded by brilliant people, men, women, his patrons admiring or perhaps chasing his commissioned works. We can almost see him, his interest jumping from one thing to another, unable to just stop and be there, unable to be present. He was incapable of keeping some sort of presence in the moment but he was always one step ahead, planning his next invention, developing his next theory, questioning himself and others on a multiplicity of facts and theories. No wonder he would have grabbed the attention of the most interesting people at court, and perhaps even been courted by some of them.

The Renaissance was a revolutionary period which shed light on the cultural, artistic and economic panorama in Europe; it was a positive upbeat moment and artists had the chance to really find themselves, developing new skills or perhaps experimenting with new techniques, materials or different forms of art. It was a time when everything felt new, everything felt possible, the man was at the centre of his own universe and he alone was capable of changing his path, taking a new adventure perhaps, starting a new journey at a different court, or why not, as Leonardo did later on in his journey, in a different country?

Many believe that the Renaissance operated as some sort of rebirth following the darkness of the Middle Ages and that is probably why everything appeared to be much more advanced and revolutionary, as the Renaissance stood out for its beauty and for being a period of extraordinary overture towards the world, compared to the uncertainty and closure of the previous era.

Artists were proactive: they wanted to change the world with their works of art, words and scientific discoveries, they wanted to put miles between themselves and the Middle Ages. One of these people, personalities and artists was, of course, Leonardo, who never stopped learning, investigating, or questioning. It is in one of his notebooks that we get a glimpse of his continuous questioning of the world and himself; when researching the Sun, he made a note in his notebook which says 'it doesn't move'. It is almost a fact – he would never go and question the church but it is clear from his notes that he did believe in the heliocentric theory and later on, as we know from his paintings and notes, also in evolution.

Leonardo worked for the church by producing different religious works of art but could not be defined as a churchman, which is in a way a tangible proof of the freedom artists boasted at that time. With his personality being so unpredictable, he was not one of the most sought-after in the ranks of the church. He had quickly built a reputation and became famous for leaving most of his works unfinished and for not being exactly keen when it came to listening to patrons' orders regarding commissioned works. Also, he was not indoctrinated by the church – he had not received a religious education, he had not even received a classical education, he was a man who was free to learn and experiment and yes, even question what the church had been trying to disseminate.

Many believe that the Renaissance was responsible for bridging the gap between the Middle Ages and our modern-day civilisation. With the Middle Ages being often depicted as a grim era with famine and pandemics such as the Black Death being its main events, it is not a surprise that the Renaissance distinguished itself with its incredible discoveries and advancements.

The Renaissance professed a philosophy that placed men and not a god at the centre of everything: humanism. A cultural movement born in Italy, humanism had the merit of promoting the idea of man, and not God, standing at the centre of his own universe. He alone could change his destiny and take action when it came to his life.

This also meant that people, anyone really, could become the very best version of themselves in any field from education to literature, the arts and science. These ideas were quickly disseminated, thanks to the invention of the Gutenberg press. Humanism was very strong in Italy – other European countries joined only later – with the movement quickly expanding to Venice, Milan, Bologna, Ferrara and Rome. Florence was its pivotal centre and it found its maximum exposure and representation in the works of artists like Leonardo, whose *Vitruvian Man* represented a perfect bridge between God and the Earth, between what was ineffable and what wasn't.

Leonardo was not the only famous personality who established himself during the Renaissance; many others did too, including Erasmus who translated the New Testament into Greek; Galileo, an Italian astronomer who got placed under house arrest for his heliocentric views; Dante, poet, writer and author of *The Divine Comedy*; William Shakespeare; and several Italian painters including Donatello, Sandro Botticelli, Raffaello and Michelangelo.

The most interesting thing about the Renaissance was that often architecture, art and science would work together in order to produce incredible projects and works of art. It was also a time to further investigate matters that directly concerned the human body and anatomy, and Leonardo was one of the first to closely study anatomy and apply its principles to recreate the human body, as seen in the perfection of the *Vitruvian Man*. The Renaissance was also famous and had the merit of portraying people and objects as closely as possible to what they really looked like in real life while also making sure to add a touch of emotion. This powerful era was also considered as the Age of Discovery, with people leading expeditions around the world to discover things that had not been discovered before: that is how famous journeys were taken by Ferdinand Magellan, Christopher Columbus, Amerigo Vespucci, Marco Polo, Ponce de Leon, Vasco Núñez de Balboa, Hernando De Soto and other explorers.

When it came to religion, the Renaissance and, in particular, humanist philosophy started questioning, maybe for the first time in history, the role of the Roman Catholic church. The reason was very simple: with more and more people getting a better education and learning not only how to read and write but also how to interpret ideas, religion became highly scrutinised and several philosophers or personalities of the time started to question whether most of the church's famous practices were aligned with the teaching of the Bible or were just a freestyle interpretation of its highest clerical figures.

In many ways, the Renaissance was a celebration of everything that was beautiful, artistic, and a continuous party of paradise, which perfectly embodied the values and spirit of the era, something that only someone like Leonardo could give life to. This time also found its most perfect expression in personalities like Leonardo and several other characters who gave their extraordinary contribution to the world of the arts by becoming Renaissance geniuses, bringing something different or new to the arts in their own way by being similar between themselves, yet different enough to start competing with each other.

Chapter 6

Leonardo and the Sforza

Leonardo spent more than ten years with the Sforza family in Milan. Ten years of work, ten years of growing professionally, ten long years of becoming Leonardo.

Of course, his lack of focus was still a major flaw in his personality, but it was mostly due to his vibrant mind and working with such a direct, strong family helped him develop both as an artist and an engineer.

He was not just a painter and he had finally come to realise that; perhaps it was something he had always known. Ever since the cave episode from his childhood, when he had the courage to embrace fear and do something despite it, he knew there was so much more in him than just painting. It was this constant thirst and search for something that would explain the unexplainable, and something that would push him beyond that extreme point of fear.

That was perhaps one of the main reasons he moved to Milan and offered his services to the Duke of Milan, Ludovico Sforza.

Was he scared to leave Tuscany and everything he knew behind? Perhaps he was, but in perfect Leonardo style, he didn't let this fear stop him from moving forward in his life and, most importantly, in his career.

Perhaps he was looking for an adventure, something that had not been imposed by his father, like when he had brought him to Florence to work with Verrocchio, or perhaps he was motivated by financial reasons or by a thirst for independence and making a name for himself; the ambition that was inside him and would often get lost in his famous lack of focus after jumping from one project to another more attractive one. He decided to leave Florence because he was aware of his talent but most importantly of his inventive nature, and he was tired of being considered just another painter at some patron's court where he had very little say or influence.

Milan was a city like no other: vibrant, fast-paced, and full of opportunities – opportunities that had the chance to emerge particularly during the Renaissance. Milan was one of the most interesting cities during the Renaissance and, especially under the Sforza family, played an important role from both an artistic and an economic point of view as the city succeeded in prospering and specialising in both the silk and wool trade. It is also important to note that, due to its location, Milan had the chance to extend its control over surrounding areas when it came to trade businesses, which made it a rich city full of endless opportunities and potential. This was something that Leonardo quickly realised.

The Sforza were also a family like no other and it was because of them and their influence that Milan had the chance to flourish during the Renaissance in various ways including architecture, with several majestic buildings being built. These included the Castello Sforzesco and the church of Santa Maria Delle Grazie.

Hoping to find better circumstances in Milan, Leonardo moved to the city and managed to establish a strong collaboration with the Sforza family; this was a collaboration which started with a simple but effective letter which still today perfectly sums up not only Leonardo's experience and abilities but also his determination to be of service to his patrons, not necessarily by painting beautiful things but mostly by being useful to someone who could potentially appreciate his engineering inventions more.

The most interesting passage in Leonardo's letter to Sforza is the one where he carefully listed all the things he could do, sparing no details, selling himself and his skills in what is today a clear example of a Renaissance CV.

In the letter, Leonardo wrote that he had knowledge in the different fields of engineering and that he could also design war weapons. The most interesting passage of the letter is the one where he casually mentions his painting skills – he brushes them off, and in the end his painting abilities seem to have very little importance to him. He does not want to be labelled in the eyes of his potential new patron as an artist. He wanted to do more and he hoped he had found in Ludovico Sforza a patron who could both understand and appreciate that.

Leonardo probably never saw himself as a full-time painter; he was a man of many talents but more than that, he was a man of many interests, and far from being just a court artist, he knew he could make a serious difference by helping his new patron in ways other artists couldn't. Even though he was a man 'senza lettere', someone uneducated, as he often called himself, he was, most importantly, a man of science, a man who based his talent on facts, on studies, and on hours understanding how everything, and more importantly everyone, worked.

His talent and his skills made him an asset and that could not have gone unnoticed. Ludovico Sforza, the one and only, Milan's first man, ruler, and prince quickly realised that Leonardo was someone to keep close and invited him to stay at his court.

The Sforza family were originally called the Attendoli. They were farmers from the Romagna who took the name Sforza with Muzio Attendolo, founder of the family and father of Francesco, who became Duke of Milan by marriage with the daughter of Duke Filippo Maria Visconti.

There were several personalities who marked the Sforza dynasty; one of the first was Galeazzo Maria Sforza, who succeeded his father in 1466 and quickly built a reputation for being an extravagant character. Despite this, Symonds in his *Renaissance in Italy: The Age of the Despots, Volume I*, includes Galeazzo on a list of men who distanced themselves from the despotic figure of the prince. He became a highly capable ruler who focused on improving the lives of his citizens; Galeazzo, for example, chose to direct his efforts towards agriculture while also building canals for irrigation and transportation and started strong patronage which saw his court being populated with artists, writers and musicians.

Following Galeazzo's assassination, the regency was briefly taken over by his wife Bona of Savoy, the chancellor Cicco Simonetta and even more briefly by Galeazzo's son, Gian Galeazzo, who was at the time 7 years old, until Ludovico the Moor (called this because of his dark complexion; the term is 'il moro' in Italian), his uncle, took over and became the new Duke of Milan, where he reigned for over thirteen years as a regent.

Ludovico Sforza was the quintessential definition of the Renaissance. He led the Sforza dynasty during the most productive time of the Renaissance in Milan and Europe, its last ten years. He was the fourth son of Francesco I Sforza and not destined to ever become duke, which is why he was not paid much attention by his family and did not receive a strictly focused education, especially when it came to the classical languages which were customary for those born in a family of means.

That gave him the opportunity to develop knowledge in different specialisms. Ludovico had the chance to expand his interests and, particularly, focus on the arts including painting and sculpture; his teacher was the humanist Francesco Filelfo.

Ludovico also studied methods of government and warfare, something which proved particularly useful later as he went on to become the Duke of Milan. As Duke of Milan, Ludovico brought several improvements to the city; like Galeazzo, he focused on agriculture, and he also paid attention to the metal as well as the silk industry. Equally, he also gave his full attention to Milan as a city as he worked on improving its cathedral as well as its streets; even the universities of Pavia and Milan went through a flourishing period during Ludovico's time.

After his marriage with Beatrice d'Este from the house of Ferrara, Ludovico's regency became more artistic, as Beatrice was 14 years old and defined by several researchers as the little light of the Sforza court: she loved life and often organised balls and festivals. She also loved to entertain all the artists and she was the one to suggest both architect Donato Bramante and Leonardo should start working for the Sforza family.

In order to combat the expansion plans for Milan of the new King of Naples, who had allied himself with Pope Alexander, Ludovico offered free passage to the King of France so that he might attack Naples instead. It turned out to be a terrible mistake, as later the king claimed Milan as well.

Ludovico also lost Beatrice after a challenging birth, something that deeply affected him. Despite being originally interested in Isabella, Beatrice's older sister, he fell in love with Beatrice, and he considered her the love of his life; he recorded in minute detail the night of her death in a letter to his brother-in-law, Francesco Gonzaga, who ended up being married to Beatrice's sister Isabella instead.

In his letter, Ludovico went into detail about how Beatrice had been suddenly taken by pains and had given birth to a stillborn child. In his letter, Ludovico went on to talk about his grief, wishing he had died himself, and that he didn't want to see anyone, he didn't want anyone around, he didn't want to be consoled, as nothing could have ever consoled him at such a terrible time. Beatrice, who had been in good health the day before her death, had also been seen riding her chariot through the park and going inside the Dominican church; she had been full of life, and being someone who loved dancing, had also been spotted dancing before the pains started on the night of her death.

Ludovico was inconsolable. He didn't even see his children for days (they had two, Massimiliano Sforza and Francesco Sforza). Beatrice was then buried in the Certosa of Pavia. It had been Beatrice who recommended Leonardo to her husband – she was the reason that Leonardo gained favour with the Sforza and became an important character at their court.

As mentioned in his letter, Leonardo had gone to Milan hoping to offer a range of services (including bridge building), something that hit the right chord with Ludovico; once there, he also offered a wide selection of artistic services as well, perhaps inspired by Lady Sforza, which also included decorating the interiors of the Castello Sforzesco and creating costumes and stages for the different events organised at the Sforza court.

It is interesting to note that Leonardo was much more connected to Ludovico than any other patron he had. The explanations could be many; it is important to note that in his own way Ludovico was an underdog, the fourth child, someone not even his own mother had paid much attention to, someone whose education had not been taken close care of, he was not meant to become someone, yet despite the odds and because of his own intelligence and craft he became more than someone, usurping for ten years the power meant for his brother's son and working his way up. It is also important to take note that it was indirectly thanks to Ludovico that Leonardo received his first important commissions.

While working for the Sforza family, Leonardo was commissioned to paint *The Virgin of the Rocks* for the Confraternity of the Immaculate Conception and *The Last Supper* for the monastery of Santa Maria Delle Grazie. Both paintings were finished and impeccably so, but they both share a different, even more, dynamic vibe compared to the one from his earliest works.

Maybe Leonardo was more experienced; he had lived more, seen more. After all, he was working under his second patronage, and had finally reached a whole different level of artistry; in both *The Virgin of the Rocks* and *The Last Supper*, the composition is almost alive and in perfect line with Leonardo's style, which brings every single one of its characters to life; they all share an emotional tridimensionality, an expression, a strong narrative and – why not? – a secret to tell, or perhaps not to.

The Virgin of The Rocks is a painting that still remains a mystery for its different messages and interpretations. It's a double painting with two different versions, the first one currently at the Louvre in Paris, the second at the National Gallery in London. However, many believe the latter to have been painted by one of Leonardo's students under his guidance, and not by Leonardo himself.

While working for the Sforza, Leonardo received further commissions; he was commissioned to paint a Madonna and had the chance to meet Matthias Corvinus, King of Hungary and Croatia.

He was also involved in several other projects, not necessarily painting-based, including the design for a dome of the cathedral of Milan and, finally, on one of his most famous works of artistic engineering, a big equestrian monument for Ludovico Sforza; this monument, which was never even started, gained a reputation for how ambitious the original idea was. Its size was bigger than anything anyone had ever achieved. A sample in wood was created but the monument itself never saw the light of day.

Under the Sforza, Leonardo was also commissioned to paint one of the most interesting portraits he had ever produced, one of Cecilia Gallerani, or as she is better known, the *Lady with an Ermine.*

Cecilia was Ludovico's favourite mistress and, naturally, Leonardo was commissioned to do her portrait. He managed to do so by not only taking her portrait but also by attaching a number of interpretations and symbolism to her representation. The choice of portraying Cecilia with an ermine had a double meaning; the duke was nicknamed 'the white ermine' and 'ermine' is a reinterpretation of Cecilia's surname 'Gallerani'; the ermine also represents everything that is feminine and pure, qualities any Renaissance woman necessarily had to possess. In this portrait, there is also a subtle nod at the affair between Cecilia and Sforza, their relationship and the willingness to make perhaps their affair more public. The painting is an oil on board and antecedent to the *Mona Lisa*; it's one of the most iconic portraits of the time.

Leonardo makes sure to paint Cecilia as a figure of virtue; she is almost emotionless except for the smile, which, much like that of the *Mona Lisa*, could be interpreted as a sign of love towards the person standing at the opposite end of the room who is apparently receiving her full attention.

Leonardo also makes sure to confer on her an element of authority, particularly visible in the way he paints her; her hair, for example, is understated but elegant and she also wears a double veil that has the merit of exalting her delicate features. Cecilia, who was Ludovico's lover by the time she was 16, gave birth to his son when she was 20. The ermine is also an element of symbolism, something Leonardo enjoyed doing in all his works, and something not common for the time: many have speculated that the ermine could represent Ludovico Sforza, so close to Cecilia who keeps him even closer in her embrace.

It was normal for the time to have a mistress or more than one, especially for men of power, wealthy men, or as per writer Machiavelli's definition, princes. It was integral to their prestige, reputation and authority to have a legitimised family and then to also have mistresses, accepted by both the rest of the family and the wives themselves, and it was natural for these mistresses to hold an important, admirable position at court, something that Cecilia Gallerani held first as Ludovico's favourite mistress and then as the mother of their child.

Following his wife Beatrice's death, Ludovico's lucky stars started to decline. The French kept advancing, and after being betrayed by his own soldiers, he spent his last years in an underground prison cell in Loches in France.

With Ludovico Sforza being overthrown, Leonardo left Milan and started a new adventure in Venice. Once again, he was ready to leave and not look back. He could not stay too long in one place; his profession made it impossible. He was dependent on princes, wealthy men, to sustain his talent and work and he knew that every single one of his patronages had an expiration date.

He packed his bags, gathered his priceless notebooks and with some of his most trustworthy collaborators started a new chapter in his life.

Chapter 7

Leonardo, Venice and Florence

By the time he had left Milan and embarked on his adventure in Venice, Leonardo was a new man. He had started to put aside his paintbrushes. He would still pick them up, of course, from time to time, but now he was much more focused on improving his knowledge when it came to other disciplines.

Venice was just what he needed. An incredible city, full of opportunities, Venice saw an impressive wealth and power both during the Middle Ages and the Renaissance with the result of the rise of a strong merchant class who would use their wealth to work with some of the most sought-after artists of the time and positively influence the city.

In Venice, Leonardo was employed as a military architect and an engineer. In particular, he was in charge of taking care of the city itself by creating strategies and methods for defence of the city against any potential or real naval attack, something which ignited and fuelled his interest for creating and designing weapons. It was not about the awful concept of harming another human being – that is not something that Leonardo could have ever conceived – but it was mostly about the idea, and probably the ego, of being capable of creating something so functional and perfectly built from an engineering perspective.

He didn't stay in Venice long and by 1500 he had moved back to his beloved Florence where he and those closest to him went to live with the Servite monks who resided at the monastery of Santissima Annunziata. The Servite monks were a group which had formed following the war between the Ghibellines and the Guelphs in Tuscany (with the first faction supporting the Holy Roman Emperor's Emperor Maximilian I and the other one supporting the papacy). Times were difficult for the population and as poverty, disease and devastation became more and more pressing, the need for a group of people with a strong desire to change things quickly became fundamental. The concept of having artists in the city to bring beauty and some lightness during such difficult times became extremely important, particularly as it served as almost their only comfort. Who better than artists to navigate through those times and show the way, perhaps offering a different perspective on a world that was evolving so rapidly?

Originally, the Servite monks were a religious group formed by seven men belonging to Florence's wealthiest families. They used to meet regularly in the name of Mary, honouring the Mother of Jesus Christ; eventually, these wealthy men decided to leave behind their comfortable lives and establish themselves in a more secluded, remote and peaceful location headquartering in Monte Senario near Florence in Tuscany. Attracting the interest of more and more people looking to engage with the group and eventually join them, the Friar Servants of Mary became a religious order around 1247.

The monks boasted extraordinarily open minds and quickly welcomed Leonardo and those working with him, his family of apprentices and friends, supporting him in his work, discoveries and studies. While staying with the monks, Leonardo had the chance to work from a workshop where, according to different biographers, he finally had the chance to start *The Virgin and Child with St Anne* and *St John the Baptist*. These are still some of Leonardo's most interesting works of art, which were affected by spending time working at the monastery and finally exploring a more spiritual side, something he had not always had the chance or the inclination to. To many researchers, Leonardo was too much of a scientist to be considered spiritual and this is reflected in most of his works, which despite dealing with a religious theme often tend to take any biblical or spiritual message or story to a whole different level, changing location, perspective or simply the characters' appearances or intentions.

Some of these famous Leonardo traits can be found in *The Virgin and Child with St Anne*. This painting, which was probably commissioned by Louis XII as some sort of homage for the birth of his daughter Claude, remains a perfect expression of Leonardo's style, and probably to the commissioner's chagrin the painting was never delivered. The composition shows most of Leonardo's pictorial characteristics from the intersection of the three figures – St Anne, the Virgin Mary and Jesus as they stand against the beautiful landscape – to Leonardo's strong interest in nature and natural beauties, which adorn the background.

Present in the painting is also Leonardo's favourite technique, the sfumato, which gives figures a pastoral and poetic glaze, while another element which is particularly strong in other Leonardo works is the inclusion of iconography; in this particular case, the lamb represents the holy spirit.

Leonardo took different sketches of this painting and only one of the final proofs also includes the figure of John the Baptist. Despite being a religious painting which portrays members of the holy family, Leonardo seemed more interested in painting the relationship between the different characters, succeeding in establishing once again a powerful narrative: Mary sits on her mother St Anne's lap, and is the most important figure in the composition, stressing their mother-daughter relationship. Also, St Anne is looking at Mary, who is looking at her son, which again makes the mother-son relationship between the two clear.

The figure of St Anne also appears larger than Mary's to make sure that anyone who looks at the painting for the first time can grasp the difference between the two women; something which wouldn't be clear otherwise, as both figures are painted with the same young, angelic face; again, another element of Leonardo's style.

A different style and purpose envelop *St John the Baptist*. The painting was conceived by Leonardo between 1513 and 1516 and many historians believe it to be one of his last paintings; that is probably why it appears to be different than anything he had ever painted before. In Leonardo's painting, St John the Baptist looks almost feminine, which is not new as Leonardo loved to add the most delicate traits to his figures and this is something that can also be noticed in other paintings including *The Last Supper* where the delicacy of the apostles' faces has created several polemics and fuelled the gossip concerning their gender.

When it comes to St John, he is pointing towards heaven, another iconographic message which could predict the coming of Christ. The background is dark with illuminated parts that have the benefit of exalting the figure of St John even more while the gesture of raising a finger, something present in other Leonardo paintings, is not only religious but also mystical; it is something that echoes of a feeling which, far from being religious, finds its origins in being almost esoteric. The smile of St John also reminds us of the *Mona Lisa*'s smile and that is probably why it leaves us feeling uneasy, observed and anxious.

The model for this painting was Leonardo's lover and student, Salai, someone who was not only very dear to Leonardo but who has often been described as smart and reckless as well as being incredibly selfish.

After spending some time in Florence, Leonardo took to travelling again and that is when he decided to move to Imola where he met and worked under another important figure of his time, Cesare Borgia.

It is with incredibly high expectations that Leonardo goes to work with Cesare. He knows he is ready for something different, he knows that he is not the man he used to be anymore, he wants to explore, perhaps even parts of himself he hasn't had the chance to explore yet.

Finally, Leonardo believes he is mature enough but most importantly experienced enough to distinguish himself at Borgia's court, particularly for his great inventions and ideas. He feels that it's his time to emerge and what better way to do that than under Italy's most challenging and complicated family?

Chapter 8

Leonardo and the Borgia

It is not difficult to establish where it all begins. The air of the morning kissing his nose, eyes looking at the world with the curiosity only a child could ever feel, experiencing nature the way he only could experience nature, in that passionate yet detached, scientific way. He was a man who had not gone to school but he would have made nature and its beauties his teacher.

We can almost see him when young, running around in Vinci, not far from his grandparents' house, perhaps chased by his beloved uncle, being free, listening to his surroundings and their secrets, understanding the endless possibilities of the world and perhaps noticing birds for the very first time.

It is this very first encounter with nature, this very first moment experiencing birds, their movement, their wings, that makes a first impression on Leonardo. Later he would also make a note about that movement and one particular machine will grab everyone's attention, a flying machine; an interesting, highly detailed design featuring two pairs of wings, moved by what could have only been a very brave pilot, and attached to a wooden frame.

He had been obsessed with wings, their movements, their lightness ever since he was a child. It's something he had tried to introduce in *The Annunciation*, his early painting, depicting an angel with such perfect wings that you could almost see them in motion.

Leonardo's flying machine featured big bat wings, a sturdy pine structure and a perfect engineering mechanism that only a genius like Leonardo could ever conceive of. It was one of Leonardo's most interesting inventions, the design of which was based on his studies of birds. He used to buy birds at the local market so that he could set them free and watch them fly away. The machine also draws inspiration from nature and the beauties around him, from Vinci to Florence and then the rest of his world, and is, even today, his very best effort to emulate birds, their movement, and what he witnessed in his continuous, tireless studies.

In the *Codex on the Flight of Birds*, a set of notes on the studies of flight, which Leonardo began as he started his researches, he makes notes about the relationship between the centre of gravity and the centre of lifting on a bird's wing, something that helped him explore even further his flying interest; it is in his notes that Leonardo seemed to also grasp for the first time the concept of air as being fluid, perhaps giving us a very first taste of aerodynamics and gravity; his inventions, his numerous interests, his quick, intelligent, always curious mind, seem to give us a further confirmation, not that we really need one, about Leonardo being always one step ahead of everyone else.

He could forge things with literally nothing at his disposal but his very own imagination, out of his very own head, and give them shape, form and a purpose, whatever popped into his head, from the study of nature to botany, birds or even medicine, stopping from time to time to look at people, their expressions, the way they were built, how their body moved, how they spoke, smiled and then focusing on bridges, cities and architecture. There was nothing Leonardo was not interested in, hadn't studied or tried to make sense of, nothing he hadn't tried to fix with one of his revolutionary, hazardous ideas. He was a risk-taker and took pleasure in trying different things, often at the same time.

It was not always easy for him to emerge as anything but a painter – after all, that's what he had studied for with Verrocchio for all those years while staying at his studio, and why his father had taken him there in the first place.

Had he been a terrible painter, things might have been easier for him, but Leonardo could paint beautiful images of women and men and angels and the world; there was nothing he could not bring to the canvas. He was a storyteller, highly capable of crafting stories with his creations turning into precious works of art, with colours being his very own personal alphabet, which inspired many but was understood by few. He was never just a painter and tried to explain it to several patrons during meetings and in letters, he would go to extreme length to make it clear: there were many things he could do or be for these rich men, the painting was just one of them, and perhaps not even his favourite thing to do.

He went to the Sforza family and stayed there for ten years, hoping to avoid painting altogether, but we know that is not exactly how it went. He wanted to be a decision-maker, someone who could bring some practical solutions to daily problems, but that was not easily achieved.

Let's imagine for a moment how these princes, these patrons, saw Leonardo, especially compared to other artists during the Renaissance. He was someone who would come to court with a full array of ideas but with the Renaissance in full flow, many of these wealthy men, men of power, would often ask him to create something beautiful with his art, something that would satisfy their ego and the people close to them – lovers, friends, family, anyone they might have wanted to impress. Having someone who would design and paint for you and quickly turn any of your artistic ideas into reality was a luxury; having an artist at your court was something only wealthy people could afford and these men were not always interested in having endless discussions with the artists they commissioned and supported financially. The war machine, a flying bird, another machine invented by Leonardo, were not what they would necessarily expect from their protégé, and not necessarily from someone who, according to many, had such a talent when it came to painting and art.

What most people probably did not realise was that, even when it came to painting, Leonardo was much more of a scientist than an artist in that sense. Yes, his works are remembered for their beauty, the angelic faces of his figures, their expressions, but it's their narrative that always stands out in the story. It was not necessarily or often the story everyone remembered but it was always something which was narrated through his personal perspective, the way he saw the figures, where he saw that story going and in his paintings; there was always a feeling of continuity; the story doesn't end within that frame, it keeps going. It was all down to planning, meticulously, religiously planning the painting, the storyline, the personality of each and every character, what they were doing, why they were standing there if the composition was complex enough, did every character have a say, a personality, something that distinguished them from the others? Then it was about what to add differently, how to re-interpret well-known scenes, even biblical ones, how to make them more current for his time and then how to keep an eye to the future; could he make these same paintings, these same figures, timeless?

A pioneer in everything he did, Leonardo even succeeded in researching and consequently using the most interesting and advanced techniques when it came to his painting, those same techniques that many have used after him.

After years of persuading and convincing, most of these patrons finally learnt to understand Leonardo and appreciate his gifts and his incredible mind, and those unpredictable ideas eventually became useful.

Despite his genius being involved in several works of art and other projects, it is Leonardo's engineering creations that gave him the chance to distinguish himself from the other artists of the time. He was not just another artist at the court of the princes; he offered something practical, and could bring something both innovative and useful to the different cities he travelled to and worked for.

As it turns out, not all his creations would be used for the good of humanity, and, despite Leonardo professing himself against any form of violence, he ended up designing and creating several war machines, which, although they served an unethical purpose in his eyes, represent a rare example of Renaissance military technology. By working under more focused, organised patronages, under princes who were not so interested in the arts but more in the life of the city itself, or in having someone who would come up with ideas to protect their city, Leonardo managed to flourish not only as an artist but also as an inventor and an engineer.

Being a man who lived for the vibrance of the cities and working for men of character, strong men, perhaps even despots, Leonardo finally succeeded in working on several interesting projects, particularly under one of his most famous patronages, the one in the service of the infamous Borgia family.

Fascinating, smart and incredibly handsome, Cesare Borgia was the Duke of Valentinois and the son of Pope Alexander VI and his most famous mistress Vanozza Cattanei. He was the oldest of his father's children with his mother (the others being Juan, Lucrezia and Jofre). Despite not having a religious inclination, he was forced to go for a career in the church as it was customary for the second son in a family; his father already had another son with another mistress, which left Cesare with no choice but to join the church. Appointed cardinal in 1493, Cesare became an important figure in his father's exclusive circle, one of his most trusted and prominent advisers. Despite this, he was not greatly loved or appreciated as he did not have a reputation for his religious vocation but rather for his hunting parties, several affairs and a predilection for expensive, luxury fashion, something he shared with Leonardo, who could not afford such luxury but who had an eye for great prints and fabrics.

Cesare and his family spent most of their lives in Spain, where his half-brother Pedro Luis was Duke of Gandía. He also received a strong Spanish education, studying with Catalan tutors including Paolo Pompilio and Giovanni Vera. According to several researchers, he was a brilliant, intelligent man.

He also went to university, attending the University of Perugia where he studied law and then the University of Pisa where he had the chance to study with Filippo Decio. In 1492, he was made archbishop of Valencia. It was his father's ascension to power and his election as Pope that gave Cesare the power he so craved. He became one of his father's most trustworthy advisers, yet he was not particularly interested in the religious life, and rather in money, power and relationships. When Pedro Luis died in 1488, Cesare's younger brother Juan was made the new Duke of Gandía and commander of the papal army. Cesare was, according to many, incredibly jealous of his brother and when Juan was murdered, Cesare became one of the prime suspects. Despite this, no proof was found against him and he was never charged.

Cesare later married Charlotte d'Albret, sister of the king of Navarre, establishing a coalition with the French, and he received from Louis XII, the French king, the title of Duke of Valentinois. In 1499, Cesare, as a captain of the papal army, started the occupation of cities which were not under the control of his father, the Pope. These included Imola and Forlì but later even Rimini, Pesaro, and Faenza; this campaign granted him and his father a reputation for being astute yet with almost no morals, and that attracted some criticisms from other Italian states as well as the other papal states.

When Giuliano Della Rovere became Pope Julius II, he decided not to confirm Cesare as a captain of the church and Duke of Romagna. Cesare was then arrested but fled to Naples, where he was arrested once more and imprisoned in the castle of Chinchilla near Valencia and then at Medina del Campo.

Leonardo's relationship with the Borgia was as interesting as it was challenging. Leonardo had high expectations when it came to his new patronage. He was prepared, as we can see from a note he made about the things he had packed when working for the Borgia, which included a pair of compasses, a sword belt, a light hat, a book of white paper, and a vest, among many other things.

While working for the Borgia, Leonardo was first asked to go to Piombino where he inspected the forts under Borgia control; he then joined Cesare in Urbino and then Pavia where he was issued a passport by Cesare himself. It's this passport that signals a shift in Leonardo's career and life. In the passport, far from being defined as a painter, Leonardo is called a military engineer and an innovator, something that he must have widely preferred, something he must have been secretly (or maybe not so secretly) proud of.

If Leonardo was a man full of life, sarcastic and ironic, Cesare was defined by Machiavelli as a man of mood swings; someone who could be secretive and quiet or full of life and words. Sometimes he went through intense days of activity where he would join in with the local sports, and others of deep depression. According to Machiavelli, he had big plans but his interests were more scientific than artistic and he employed Leonardo as his inspector of fortresses but never commissioned him with any artistic works.

Machiavelli, a strong admirer of Cesare Borgia, defined him as possessing all the qualities a prince must necessarily possess including being aggressive, ruthless and opportunistic; qualities Cesare did not fail to show, especially when he decided to expand the papal territories into a bigger central state, including Romagna.

But where did Leonardo fit into all this? Leonardo was the engineer of the plan, the man Cesare had envisioned to build war machines and bridges and subdue the cities that were still not ready to fall under the Borgia family's power, and that is exactly what Leonardo did. By the summer of 1502, he was inspecting Piombino and its fortifications, drawing maps and assisting Cesare in everything he desired. No one said no to Cesare Borgia, no one would have dared.

The figure of Cesare has always been a challenging, complicated one. He always seemed to stand right at the centre of important, interesting and somewhat reputation-tainting rumours which included the murder of his brother Juan – guilty, according to many, of having by-passed him for the title of Duke of Gandía – and his incestuous relationship with his sister Lucrezia, who was very beautiful. Despite this, Cesare still managed to survive, at least politically, by succeeding in marrying Charlotte and consequently receiving the title of Duke of Valentinois.

According to writer and diplomat Machiavelli, Cesare was a man who had no effective interest in the arts; he was not particularly taken by artists and could not see the use of working with artists to produce any form of artistic creation, and that is probably why, while under his patronage, Leonardo da Vinci was not commissioned with any artistic work.

Not that Leonardo was interested in the first place, or was particularly disappointed with that; when it came to his time at the Borgia court, Leonardo had other ideas and plans, and these certainly didn't involve using his paint brushes anytime soon. Finally, he had found what he had always looked for, someone who would understand him, cherish his work, give him the support he needed and treat him with the respect someone like him, who was so much more than an artist, really deserved.

It is with this mindset that Leonardo approached his work under the patronage of the Borgia. With Cesare, Leonardo had the invaluable chance to experiment with different interests and explore his studies further, particularly covering anything that really appealed to him; these interests included military architecture. He and Cesare also travelled throughout Italy together and it is probably during this time that Leonardo started nurturing a strong interest in towns and succeeded in adding town planning to his CV, something that he was particularly keen to develop.

The idea of town planning was created out of necessity, something he had been obsessing over for a very long time and had the potential to bring some important, visible improvements to people and the way they used and interacted with their surroundings on a daily basis.

He started to work on the creation of the perfect city, an ideal place, an idea born out of pure and simple necessity which had been influenced by the pestilence of 1486; something so cruel and devastating that had deeply impacted Milan and slaughtered half its population.

It was this tragic event that had pushed Leonardo to have a serious think about cities and work on how to improve them and create better-equipped ones for people. Far from staying in his notes, Leonardo followed through with this particular concept by working on large-scale projects which included the reconfiguration of Pienza and the expansion of Ferrara; these projects brought Leonardo to question the way medieval cities were built and how overcrowded streets had become; there were too many habitations being built in not enough space, and moving forward, this would not be the most effective solution.

It is in the Paris Manuscript B and the Codex Atlanticus that we can trace back Leonardo's passion for urban planning and his interest and thoughts which particularly concerned the creation of a new city along the Ticino river. In his works, Leonardo often talks about the creation of a comfortable and big enough city, with strong walls, and he also goes as far as adding articulated plans for this ideal city which, in his opinion, needs to be built in a different way. Structured on several levels obtained by the use of vertical staircases, Leonardo's ideal city looked eccentric for the time but, as with most of Leonardo's projects, inventions or just ideas, also almost futuristic. Also in his notes, we can see how Leonardo planned to add artificial canals throughout the city so that it would be easier for boats to transport goods, proving once again that he was always one step ahead.

Under Cesare Borgia's patronage, Leonardo managed to create a map of Cesare's property and a town plan of Imola, and, as a consequence of this, Cesare decided to make him his chief military engineer and architect. This was the beginning of everything he had ever dreamt of; to be recognised as an engineer and an architect must have been the satisfaction he had been waiting for, perhaps, his entire life. In many ways, it gave Leonardo that sense of purpose he had been yearning for since he was a child; he was a man who had built himself up from scratch, working on his education, learning from others, from his surroundings, from nature itself, and he had done such a wonderful job that now someone like Cesare Borgia would actually nominate him his first man when it came to matters of engineering and architecture.

When it came to town planning, Leonardo wasn't done, and later he also worked on the design of a map of the Chiana Valley in Tuscany.

While working for Cesare, Leonardo had the chance to experiment with plenty of his own ideas and finally put to the test some of his best theories regarding his most dangerous inventions. These particularly involved war inventions and especially concerned the design of war machines that were both defensive and offensive, something that can still be found in his notes.

When it came to war machines, they were not something that he would create in the heat of the moment but always as a product of time and research during the years; studying, researching and testing, perhaps, some of the less deadly ones.

One of his most famous inventions was a 33-barreled organ, a machine whereby the gun could be loaded and fired at the same time. An interesting, revolutionary concept, particularly for Leonardo's era and made possible thanks to an easy to rotate mechanism which allowed soldiers to quickly reload the guns. The 33-barreled organ was an invention that stood out for being both innovative and incredibly pioneering for the time. Leonardo's machine had managed to do something no one else had ever dared, to fix the issue of having to use cannons, which were too slow to load. Another war machine or device Leonardo designed was a ballista, which essentially constituted a big crossbow which would throw large stones and flaming bombs, something quite interesting as, despite being an offensive tool, it also had a double purpose which was to cause panic and intimidate the enemy.

To understand Leonardo and his connection to Cesare, it is necessary to consider their relationship and its timing. The patronage of the Borgia came at a time when Leonardo finally had the confidence to go for a life that was not necessarily dictated by what he knew and where he came from, a life shaped according to where he intended to go and who he intended to be. He was not just another illegitimate child whose parents did not bother to take care of him and whose love he clearly missed. Like Sforza, to some extent, Cesare gave him what he needed: a title, his full attention and his interest. Leonardo must have felt flattered to see that title written clearly on paper, to be appointed as an engineer, to receive that level of attention and appreciation for the very first time perhaps in his life.

For a man who had no formal education, to be able to access such a sought-after court must have been the highlight of his career; furthermore, this created a ripple effect of possibilities, the endless possibilities that the Borgia created for him out of thin air: travelling, the chance to craft, to design new machines, war machines, but also the opportunity to draw maps and think about the city, and how to be of use to Borgia's dreams of power and expansion.

Despite never being commissioned with any works of art, Leonardo drew Cesare on a number of occasions, in sketches found in his notebooks, where life really happened, or anything worth noting was carefully frozen in time for anyone to read and find out more about later. In Leonardo's sketches of Cesare, there are no names or further explanations. Leonardo draws a Borgia who is older and perhaps not as handsome anymore; as people have reported, Cesare's beauty and charisma preceded him and have also been represented in various dramatisations for films and TV.

Leonardo's drawings and sketches do not convey that level of beauty and almost perfection that Cesare was so famous for; we can see a tired version of Cesare Borgia as seen through Leonardo's lens. He was perhaps not exactly the prince Machiavelli portrayed in his works, but ended up as, or perhaps he always was, a man whose dreams had turned him into one of the most fascinating characters of the Renaissance.

Cesare Borgia was one of the most important personalities of the Renaissance in Italy; he was a prince, a man of power, a man of means, someone who was used to having everything he wanted, every woman he wanted, including, as many believe, his own sister Lucrezia.

Movies and TV series have talked extensively about the Borgia, as a powerful, mysterious and often purportedly immoral family, a trait that did not necessarily only concern Cesare and his relationship with his sister, but also his alleged participation at the Banquet of Chestnuts (an orgy involving fifty prostitutes and members of the clergy that was rumoured to be hosted by Cesare Borgia himself). One thing is sure, it was the relationship with his family and his sister which made him an attractive, mysterious figure in the history of the Renaissance.

In our collective imaginary, often supported by film and TV representations, Lucrezia and Cesare have been endlessly romanticised. He has always been portrayed as a protective, masculine type while she has almost always been dramatised as a temptress, someone no one could trust.

Yet this version of her being some kind of villain does not sit well with most historians and researchers as this is not necessarily the most accurate portrait we have of her.

Many believe that Lucrezia Borgia was a prey, a victim of her family, someone who was abused to the point of neglect, violence and perhaps rape. She was probably not as strong as she has been shown to be; she was manipulated and used in a game of power by her brother and her father alike. In order to satisfy their expansion dreams, they often used Lucrezia, marrying her off to different men, older or younger than her, it really didn't matter. In a patriarchal time, she was just a woman and, despite being a woman of power, she was not often taken into consideration, not even when it came to things that involved her directly.

How did Leonardo feel about the Borgia family and about both Cesare and Lucrezia? We know that Cesare was probably one of the first princes to recognise in Leonardo something that went above and beyond his painting skills, which must have given Leonardo a sense of being in constant debt towards his new patron. Cesare had been the one to grant him a different role in the society of the time, the role of a genius, engineer, someone who was not purely an artist or a painter; but did Leonardo manage to distinguish between his own admiration for Cesare and the way he treated his own sister? And see him clearly for who he was?

When it came to Lucrezia, Leonardo was probably not impressed by the way she was treated by her family and how much they would use, abuse and quickly dispose of her. By this time, we know that Leonardo was a keen observer of life; he noticed things before anyone else and despite rarely expressing an opinion which could upset his patrons, current and former, he would take a step back, or fail to finish a project, rather than being openly vocal about it.

He never expressed himself against the Borgia, yet he kept working on war machines for the princes of the time. He never addressed the rumours which circulated about the family, something which he certainly knew. He worked with Cesare and enjoyed being at his service, perhaps one of his most important men, yet he never took a full, official portrait of him, or of anyone in his family, including Lucrezia, who never became one of his muses.

There is so much noise in the things Leonardo did not talk about. Was this some sort of silent protest against Cesare and his family? Many historians noticed that Leonardo hardly ever produced any artistic work while with the Borgia; he was never commissioned to, and all we have left is a couple of sketches of Cesare and Lucrezia, portrayed by Leonardo as a creature of beauty, dignity and far from being the temptress everyone else described.

Lucrezia Borgia was another important character and impressive figure in the Borgia family. Like Cesare, she was the daughter of Pope Alexander VI and Vanozza Cattanei; she did not boast a great reputation and was often associated with her family's crimes. She had three marriages with influential and highly sought men in the society of the time. She was highly educated and spoke Italian, French, Latin and Greek. She married very early, when she was only a teenager, and her first husband, Giovanni Sforza, was fifteen years older than her. He was the Lord of Pesaro and Count of Catignola. Her first marriage was later annulled as not being consummated but that was not the real reason; the truth was that her brother and father had changed their minds and decided that her marriage to Sforza was not politically convenient to the Borgia. They didn't care that, at the time, Lucrezia was pregnant and had to be sent to a convent to give birth. Different sources claim that the child was not a product of her marriage with Sforza but rather the illegitimate child of her brother Cesare or even her father Rodrigo.

Lucrezia later married Alfonso of Aragon, Duke of Bisceglie and Prince of Salerno of the House of Trastámara, who was only 17 at the time of the marriage. The two had a child together but Alfonso was later killed by Cesare as he sought an alliance with France. Cesare was particularly concerned that Alfonso and the Kingdom of Naples could have been a problem to his expansion dreams in the long run, as Alfonso was the illegitimate son of Alfonso II King of Naples and his mistress Trogia Gazzella. Later, Lucrezia was married to Alfonso d'Este, Duke of Ferrara, marking a new beginning in her life and a detachment from her family schemes and rumours alike. With Alfonso and Lucrezia becoming Duke and Duchess of Ferrara, Lucrezia finally had a chance to become a patron of the arts as well as a strong personality in the artistic community in Ferrara.

Later in her life, she also turned to religion following the death of her son, Rodrigo, and sadly died in childbirth at the age of 39.

Lucrezia and Cesare had a strong relationship, something powerful that had an impact on both their lives, yet they were most certainly not the easiest patrons to work for. Following his experience with Cesare Borgia, Leonardo found himself changed; he saw what war did to human beings, those same human beings he would study for his paintings. He was so profoundly and deeply affected by the experience of working with Cesare that he felt there was very little he could do in his service anymore.

It is at this time that Leonardo makes a shift, not in his beliefs but perhaps in his attitude. It is at this time that he finally realises that he cannot work with people like Cesare anymore. He is an inventor, he is someone who has ideas on a whim but he is not someone who can condone war in any form. He is a Renaissance man and not someone who will use his talent, his genius and his ideas to kill other men. It is with this spirit, with his dreams of glory shattered that Leonardo decides or is more likely forced to leave the famous Borgia behind in favour of something different.

He knows he cannot change the world but he also knows he cannot stay there, he cannot keep working for the Borgia. Once again, there is only one place that feels like home to him and that place is Florence.

Chapter 9

Leonardo, Florence Again

He decided to go back to Florence, to his Florence, trying to find himself perhaps, trying to find something that would give his soul some sense of inspiration. He gradually immersed himself once again in the Florentine world, the one that had originally given him a profession, a purpose in life, and that is how he found himself being commissioned to do what will be Leonardo's most interesting (yet never even started) work of art: *The Battle of Anghiari*. Many researchers define *The Battle of Anghiari* as the result of what he had seen with the Borgia, proof of everything he had learnt to detest and of what he would never touch again.

It is interesting to note that it had taken someone like Cesare Borgia to make Leonardo abandon his war inventions obsession; he never condoned war but he had probably never seen with his eyes the horror that war could leave behind, and he decided not to be a part of it, not playing a role with his ideas, inventions or notes in it, not anymore.

He knew he had to move on, once again, he knew his time with Cesare had finally come to an end and there was nothing else he could do there. In October 1503, Leonardo moved again, packed his things, and with his favourite students, now turned friends, some of them lovers, he decided to leave Cesare behind in his belligerent world, and move back to Florence.

He needed to find himself again and there was no better city, no better place that could have made him feel better after the horrors he had experienced with the Borgia.

He counted on stopping for a while in Florence, recharging and then perhaps in better times finding another patron, someone interested in his work, in what he had to offer, and moving again.

He knew he was not made to stay in any place for too long; he knew that eventually he would grow bored of Florence as well but for the time being, that was exactly what he needed.

In Florence, he made sure to join the Guild of Saint Luke again, and it is here that Leonardo starts a portrait, or perhaps *the* portrait, the one that will change his life and consecrate both him and his work in the history of art as timeless icons. It is at this time in his life that Leonardo succeeds in creating an icon that still today intrigues millions of people: the icon in question takes the shape of Lisa del Giocondo, believed to be the model for the *Mona Lisa*.

The *Mona Lisa* is the mysterious painting that was commissioned perhaps by Lisa's husband but never delivered; it's iconic, beautiful, yet something Leonardo only manages to start once he is back in Florence. It is almost as though the proximity to his favourite city and being so close to home has the merit of awakening him; his humour, his love for life, something that he had perhaps lost a little when working under the patronage of Cesare Borgia. In many ways, it is in the *Mona Lisa*'s smile that Leonardo finds his way again and perhaps even himself.

Following the creation of his most interesting portrait, Leonardo begins a new phase. Painting and art are back in his life, perhaps the consequence of being back in Florence, a city which was the epitome of the Renaissance itself.

It is at this time that he decides to embrace a brand new commission, something that at first makes him incredibly excited; it is a mural painting about *The Battle of Anghiari* for the Signoria; the commission is going to work in partnership with Michelangelo who, at the same time, or shortly after, is supposed to design *The Battle of Cascina*. The two artists are mortal enemies, competitors, who do not like to be in the same room for too long, so from the very beginning the whole project is doomed.

We also know that both paintings will never be completed. Leonardo never manages to finish his painting because of several technical problems, particularly involving the use of a different colour technique; something that would leave him in utter despair.

His work, his entire plan for *The Battle of Anghiari*, is something that would only make an appearance in his notebooks, with his sketches and ideas giving us an initial sample of the majestic work of art he had in mind from the very beginning.

It is unclear why Michelangelo, a rival of Leonardo who often accused him of being unreliable and never completing his paintings or any work, did not finish his own painting. Many researchers believe that he was called to Rome to work on a different commission. As acclaimed and loved as both painters were, it is interesting that neither of them succeeded in what would have been a painting of titanic magnitude from the point of view of dimension, style and technique.

While staying in Florence, Leonardo also started to write the Codex Atlanticus, researching, studying, often staying up late at night. The Codex is a collection of twelve volumes which explore Leonardo's mind, looking at his interests, research studies and covering a wide range of topics.

Covering his entire career, the Codex Atlanticus takes its name from Leonardo's use of large white sheets comparable to geographic atlases. This incredible portfolio of works has the purpose of showcasing Leonardo's sketches of some of his best inventions including parachutes, war machines and even hydraulic pumps. Leaving very little to the imagination, Leonardo writes, draws and takes notes on some of his most brilliant ideas. The Codex also has some of his best sketches following his architectural and anatomy studies, particularly following his cadaver dissection practice, something that led him to understand human beings and their nature even more.

As anticipated, his time in Florence didn't last. He was a traveller, someone who liked to move around, meet people, learn from them, and he never stayed too long in the same place. His home was the people he would often take with him, his students, his family, those who were the closest to him, who served both as inspiration and often as models for his paintings.

By 1506, Leonardo was asked by Charles II d'Amboise, who was the French Governor of Milan during the reign of Louis XII, to join him in Milan.

He left Florence, despite protests; everyone wanted him to finish his work, everyone there wanted him to finally do what he had promised, finish his mural painting, find a way to finally paint the masterpiece he had promised to complete. They tried, they almost forced him to finish *The Battle of Anghiari*, but it was all in vain, and this was added to Leonardo's collection of unfinished works.

The time had come again to leave. Leonardo decided to join the court of Louis XII, who was a big fan of his art and his genius and had commissioned him to do some portraits which gave him the perfect chance not only to take some time off in Florence but also to work on his art again, start afresh.

From Milan, Leonardo moved briefly back to Florence. Many researchers and biographers believe that in 1507 Leonardo was in Florence because of his father's death, to take care of matters concerning his will, although it is ascertained that Piero, Leonardo's father, left nothing to him, not even bothering to recognise him as his son, even after his death.

This brought issues when it came to the matter of Piero's will as Leonardo did not receive anything. Later, when his uncle Francesco died, Leonardo was stated as the only beneficiary of his will, which included a house Leonardo himself had improved for his uncle, supporting him financially during the years.

Even then, his brothers wanted to stop him from getting his inheritance and started legal procedures which dragged for a long time. In the end, both parties settled, with Leonardo finally receiving Francesco's house but only with the agreement that, at his death, the house would return to his family. Later, around 1508, he briefly returned to Milan, a city he had always admired and felt at home in, and where he lived in his own house in Porta Orientale in Santa Babila.

However, he was not the same Leonardo. He was a different man, a more experienced one, he had worked with different patrons, princes, despots alike, men who would make the history of the Renaissance. Their opinions, their words, their influence had a strong mark, almost a hold on him, yet even that phase was over now: he was ready for the next one in his life. He had created, designed and lived under the patronage of these men, learning about their lives, bringing something different to their patronage, government, perhaps to the way they ruled. The new phase of his life would be less proactive, less focused on pleasing the princes in his life and perhaps exploring a different side of himself, exploring the reason why he had started this journey of discovery in the first place; there was no more time to dream.

Or perhaps it was time to dream of something else, and France could have been the perfect way to action that plan. He needed a different patron, he was getting old, he needed someone who could see his genius but leave him free, independent enough to continue his study without pestering him with more commissions.

A new phase in his life was starting, a different one, he had finally become one of the most sought-after artists in Italy, a genius, someone who was appreciated by many and deeply, passionately loved by just as many extraordinary artists and people of the time. A few of these would end up becoming some of his most famous lovers, others his competitors.

Chapter 10

Leonardo, the Competitor

Leonardo was a sensitive man. Perhaps too sensitive – he feared other people's judgement, he was sensitive to their opinion of him, of what they might say about him, perhaps when he was not there. An interesting passage from his notebooks explains how someone who was not named had had the audacity to go to his friends and patrons (people dear to Leonardo who had managed to keep objective and wise despite being told untruths about him) and spread lies about him, aimed at his person. It is the first time, perhaps, that Leonardo, the maestro, someone always depicted as a genius, as a man who was always above and beyond everything and everyone else, shows something that we have never seen before: vulnerability.

He was a man who was capable of being over-sensitive, and perhaps a modern Renaissance over-thinker, who was very much living in his own head, his conscience, something that would later be explored by one particular film (*Io, Leonardo*), playing an important role in his life.

Despite many depicting Leonardo as this perfect, almost unreal creature, he was far from it; he was a man and, like most men, he was no stranger to jealousy and competitions. The society of the time did not help and a patronage system based on preferences did nothing to alleviate a general feeling of profound inadequacy; he was always out of place, and perhaps never really home. This was something Leonardo had already experienced during his childhood, something that had been reflected in many of his early experiences from growing up almost without a mother figure, someone who had soon recreated a new family which had not included him, to being the firstborn but illegitimate son of a father who was not interested in his upbringing, someone who was not there for him. It is during this uncertainty that Leonardo first had to deal with feelings of insecurity.

All of these circumstances might have amplified a sense of inadequacy as well as a passion for knowledge in order to counteract that. Yes, Leonardo was a man of many talents, but he perhaps became a genius, a legend and a researcher to satisfy that thirst for knowledge and perhaps to prove something to others, those who received better opportunities in life, those who had perhaps studied Latin and Greek, those who had received a standard education, something that he had not.

It is during these times and within a patronage framework that used to pit artists against one another, and which was essentially based on favouritism, that Leonardo found himself having to fight to gain the attention of the prince, of the patron, no matter which one. The prince was the only one who could grant him access to funds in order to help him with his inventions, with his incredible yet expensive ideas, bringing to life what he only had the courage to dream on paper.

Imagine the beautiful courts, the one of the Medici, the one of the Sforza and then the one of the Borgia. Leonardo was there, having to constantly prove his worth, his value, having to constantly prove his talent, the validity of his ideas but also their practicality, trying to find a place at court, featuring alongside some incredible men and artists of his time, having to better them, having to better himself, showing princes that he, Leonardo, was the only one they needed, the only one who could give them so much more than aesthetically beautiful works of art – he could give them power, knowledge, by only picking one idea from his notebooks: they needed no other artists at their court, they had a genius.

Princes, patrons, had a tendency of having a favourite, someone they felt they had a better connection with, or perhaps only someone who would be a bit more flexible when it came to the commission, someone who would finish his commissioned work on time or would be happy to work the way the patron demanded in the first place, perhaps even listening to them when it came to material choice or painting style. Leonardo was nothing like that; he was a rebel, he didn't listen much to his patrons, he didn't like to be told what to do, wasn't exactly happy to spend his time painting, or even to be treated like an artist. He was so much more, and that is probably why he didn't end up being a favourite at the court of the Medici, or later on, when he moved to Rome, why he could do nothing against Raffaello Sanzio, a rival, a wonderful painter and a competitor. Raffaello was not the only competitor though, as, throughout his whole career, Leonardo managed to get himself a few more, some of them just as talented and incredibly famous.

Leonardo and Michelangelo

It's a very hot day during what it looks like a suffocating Italian summer, and soldiers are bathing in the Arno to escape the heat and try to freshen up after another long day at the front. Someone, the Florentine captain perhaps, raises a false alarm, he doesn't want his troops to slack and, by doing so, being caught off guard by the enemy. In a second everyone rushes to dress, some are still in the water, others already brandishing arms. It's a messy, chaotic moment from *The Battle of Cascina*, which was a preliminary drawing by Michelangelo and celebrates the victory of Florence over Pisa.

This drawing was supposed to be a magnificent painting as Michelangelo was commissioned to work on the wall of the Palazzo Vecchio next to Leonardo's *Battle of Anghiari*; another painting which also remained unfinished.

Leonardo and Michelangelo had a challenging relationship from the very beginning. They were both highly sought after and successful artists of the time yet they didn't like each other very much. According to Vasari, they felt pure and simple dislike for each other, but he never fully explained why. Many other researchers and biographers strongly believe that their dislike was caused by Michelangelo, whose jealousy could hardly stand anyone even daring to talk about Leonardo.

There is a popular episode which perfectly sums up their rivalry. One day, a group of people asked Leonardo as he was passing through the Piazza Santa Trinità in Florence to explain a passage from Dante. Michelangelo, who was walking nearby, was cornered by Leonardo and pressured to explain the passage instead. Michelangelo didn't let Leonardo humiliate him and, in exchange, accused him of being an unreliable artist who had made a sketch of a bronze horse but who had never seen the project through to the end; the horse in question was the big equestrian monument Leonardo had planned and begun in Milan for the Sforza family. Once again, something he had left unfinished.

This majestic monument, something so beautiful, something so impressive that everyone had been talking about for years – where was it now? Michelangelo must have asked Leonardo in order to embarrass him instead.

He had humiliated Leonardo openly and with some of their acquaintances as his audience. He had succeeded in wounding Leonardo where he was weaker; taking a hit at Leonardo's legendary unreliability, which had become almost as famous as he was. Perhaps Michelangelo couldn't quite understand why Leonardo had been called a genius for so many years, what it was about him that made everyone so confident about his talent, about his impressive ideas, why someone who clearly lacked practicality in his inventions or sketches was so sought-after and boasted such a great reputation for being a master in everything he did. He had aimed to discredit Leonardo and his work, reminding everyone of his biggest failure. Leonardo had, according to Michelangelo, failed at being an artist, a sculptor worth consideration, certainly in his eyes, but mostly in the eyes of the Renaissance group of artists and people of means, the patrons, those who really counted. He really wanted to taint Leonardo's reputation even more, and jealousy could be one of the many reasons he decided to do so.

Leonardo did not like Michelangelo and that was also apparent. After all, it was Leonardo who had, at first, challenged Michelangelo, asking him to express his thoughts on a passage from Dante. It is interesting how they bickered between themselves and how many historians believe that it wasn't the first time that they had engaged in such a public display of animosity. Leonardo was in no way a victim, and when it came to establishing the collocation of Michelangelo's beautiful statue, *David*, he had been the one, according to different researchers, to suggest it be installed somewhere a little less renowned than Palazzo Vecchio in Florence.

There could be many reasons explaining why Michelangelo had been so direct in questioning the talent and the skills of Leonardo as an artist. Was he as jealous of Leonardo as many believed? Or perhaps he had just got upset after learning that Leonardo did not like his painting style, according to Vasari's notes?

There is a chance that their rivalry started as they both went to make a name for themselves in Florence around 1504, when the Medici controlled the city, its art scene and of course, its artists; many sources believe that both artists were often pitted against each other. At the time, they were both highly successful and skilful and they may not have liked being compared or even considered to be in the same group of successful Renaissance artists and figures of importance and talent. Michelangelo, for instance, was one of the most appreciated artists of the Renaissance and even Vasari sang his praises in his biographies, defining him as one of the best artists, if not the best. Michelangelo was an appreciated artist and many believed that his artistry would go beyond Italy, making him one of the most interesting and revolutionary personalities of his time and perhaps ours. He also stood out not only for his talent but also for his extraordinary discipline when it came to his works, often producing several commissions at the same time. There are many theories about how the animosity between the two masters began; many believe that it all started when Michelangelo's assistant Condivi forgot to add Leonardo while drafting his master's biography, an innocent mistake or, perhaps, something more than that.

The two artists were obviously very different. Leonardo was a creative genius and soul, open to the world and others, while Michelangelo was a little more closed, his personality a little harsher and more distant. Leonardo was often found at court, walking around, talking to patrons about his ideas, what he could do better, how he could improve what he had already done; he was eclectic, enjoyed experimenting with different projects at the same time, he was musical, he was a scientist and he rarely ever finished any work. Michelangelo was also a polymath but in a different way; he was highly critical of himself and of the society of the time, he was not as open as Leonardo when it came to the world and others.

He also had terrible habits when it came to personal hygiene and it is rumoured that he would never wash or change clothes. Legend says that when he died these had to be cut and delicately peeled off him. Leonardo was the opposite – he apparently had a strong fashion sense and he wouldn't dream of going out in public wearing something ugly, let alone dirty.

Michelangelo was also not new to animosity when it came to rival painters. It is interesting to note that his commission for the Sistine Chapel started out as a form of sabotage from Raffaello; the latter, who had been commissioned first to paint the chapel, ended up suggesting Michelangelo as a way to prove to his patron Pope Julius II, with whom he was losing favour, that Michelangelo was not a painter but just a sculptor. The Sistine Chapel was a triumph and Michelangelo proved that he was not only an excellent sculptor but also a talented painter; legend also tells that Michelangelo was bitter with Raffaello because he had lost a duel against him.

Notes found later about his work on the Sistine Chapel show that Michelangelo himself didn't consider himself a painter, even writing the words, 'I am not a painter.'

Was Michelangelo so averse to Leonardo because he recognised in him a talent for painting that he, strangely enough, didn't perceive he had himself? Despite not considering himself a painter and categorically not wanting to be labelled as a painter, Leonardo boasted of a wonderful reputation for his painting technique 'the sfumato' and for the delicacy of his angelic figures. Perhaps this was one of the reasons why Michelangelo did not particularly like Leonardo.

Michelangelo was one of the most appreciated artists of his time; he was a sculptor, a painter, a poet and even an architect. Unlike Leonardo, Michelangelo came from an aristocratic family who had lost everything by the time he was born. His father was an administrator of the town of Caprese who was not a big fan of his son's artistic dreams. He probably didn't see in him a talent and was not interested in supporting him from that point of view, and that is probably the reason why Michelangelo started his apprenticeship quite late for the time; he was 13 when he finally started his career as an apprentice working for the painter Domenico Ghirlandaio. At first, he tried to learn as much as he could, but the relationship did not go quite as planned. Michelangelo was a young artist, someone who had never received an artistic education and was new to this world. Despite this, after only a few months of apprenticeship with Ghirlandaio, it became apparent that he was incredibly gifted, and that is probably why he decided that his new master had nothing to teach him and left for a new adventure.

Ghirlandaio was not the master he had sought, the one who could teach him something new and innovative when it came to painting or art in general; he found him extremely outdated and decided to move on to find his luck somewhere else. In comparison, Leonardo stayed at Verrocchio's for a very long time, not because he was learning anything new in particular but mostly for the affection that he had towards his master; he only later became independent and started his own studio.

Unlike Leonardo, Michelangelo soon became one of Lorenzo de' Medici's favourite painters. He was so talented that he found no difficulties finding the favour of the Magnifico. Michelangelo also had a certain reliability that Leonardo so obviously lacked; under his patronage, he had the chance to really explore his talent, perhaps for the very first time since he had come to Florence, starting a new artistic profession he knew almost nothing about. Following the Medici family being overthrown, Michelangelo decided to move again, and this time he took an even more adventurous step, moving to a whole different city, Bologna.

It was in Bologna that Michelangelo started his work as a sculptor. He began carving small figures to complete the tomb and shrine of St Dominic, a small project but one that certainly had the merit of finally proving to himself and others that he had a predilection for sculpting as well as a talent for it. Even the St Dominic commission was not intended for him and was only given to Michelangelo following the original sculptor's death. After this very first project, Michelangelo also briefly returned to Florence, where he completed a statue called the *Bacchus*, probably one of the most important of his life. In particular, it eventually led him to sculpt the one that would turn out to be one of the biggest commissions of his life, the *Pietà*, now in St Peter's Basilica. The *Pietà* is a devotional image which sees the Virgin Mary as she is crying over the body of Jesus Christ, the two figures skilfully extracted from one marble block.

His reputation started to precede him and he was also later on commissioned with *David* for the cathedral of Florence, the infamous statue that had a whole group of people deciding his future collocation in Florence, a group that, as we know by now, was headed by Michelangelo's rival, Leonardo. One of the most interesting things about Michelangelo's *David* is its relationship with the principles developed originally by artists from classical antiquity; Michelangelo, in fact, used perfect geometry to produce something which is still today brought as an example of a Renaissance masterpiece. Later, Michelangelo also produced several Madonnas for private collectors in the shape of both statues and paintings, as the religious theme was something which was extremely popular during the Renaissance. His most famous work remained the ceiling of the Sistine chapter, a relatively unimportant job which turned out to be one of his most beautiful works of art.

As mentioned, Leonardo and Michelangelo were not friends, yet after Leonardo came back to Florence many artists, including perhaps Michelangelo, were influenced by his work. One thing is sure, the two were incredibly different: Michelangelo was a brilliant, proactive artist who would sculpt or paint almost incessantly, who would never tire and who would see a project through to the end. Leonardo was a brilliant man but not as proactive when it came to painting. He was not interested in art as such, he was not interested in being a painter or being a commissioned artist at the dependence of a master, of a prince; he hated that sort of patronage, he wanted to bring solutions, to help people, to make life better for those he served and, despite being a genius when it came to painting, he was never as proactive as an artist. When working, for example, on incredible works of art like *The Last Supper* he was never as focused, and according to different testimonials he could be found working at the painting for whole days – he wouldn't drink, he wouldn't eat, he wouldn't stop, the painting itself became his life, and then he would go and forget about it, stare at the painting, leave it for days, maybe just adding a few touches.

According to a 2019 documentary by Alberto Angela produced by Rai, even when it came to the human body Michelangelo and Leonardo could not be more different, Michelangelo was interested in the muscles, the beauty of the human figure, its strength, while Leonardo would learn very quickly how to dissect cadavers, not for a particular interest in anything that was horrid or macabre but mostly because he was fascinated about how everything worked and how much he could learn about human beings by having a look directly inside their bodies.

But were the two jealous of each other? Was Leonardo really worried about Michelangelo's success and his fame or was he as detached as many describe him? Was this rivalry, this competition, just something in Michelangelo's head?

He had been very careful when it came to dissociating himself from those artists he thought old, outdated, less advanced, or revolutionary in their approach to the arts but could he have included Leonardo, the genius and the artist appreciated by many in this group? He questioned Leonardo's reliability as an artist several times and rightly so; Leonardo was not famous for finishing what he had started. But was this trait of his personality, this work process if you like, the only reason why Michelangelo didn't like him?

Many believe that Michelangelo was not the most amicable, sociable person while Leonardo seemed to be a luminous, positive person in comparison. They were different, that's for sure – they didn't have much in common except for the fact that they were both extraordinary artists, appreciated by important patrons including the Medici and biographers alike, despite polemics including that by Vasari.

No one knows what happened in those rooms of Palazzo Vecchio as they were both commissioned to work on its walls; only those walls know about their rivalry, about how much they hated each other, about how Leonardo was jealous of Michelangelo, someone whose praises had been sung everywhere, and how Michelangelo was jealous of Leonardo, the master, the genius, the one whose beauty, talent and intelligence attracted and captivated everyone he met. Many researchers believe that Leonardo escaped to France so that he did not have to talk to, see or even hear about Michelangelo. They were so different yet so similar and, as it turned out, both their paintings about battles, those of Anghiari and Cascina, both commissioned for Palazzo Vecchio, remained unfinished, leaving us only with the idea, the dream of what it could have been.

Leonardo and Raffaello

Raffaello Sanzio was a master painter who, much like Leonardo, was one of the most interesting characters of the Renaissance. He was born in 1483 in Urbino and he was the son of Giovanni Santi and Maria di Battista di Nicola Ciarla. His father was, according to Vasari, a painter of no particular talent or merit but he succeeded in giving Raffaello a start when it came to basic painting techniques and humanistic philosophy. Raffaello is also mostly remembered for his Madonnas and for his large compositions in the Vatican.

Much like Leonardo and Vinci, Raffaello's place of birth Urbino had a deep influence on his art; later he would also be inspired by other artists and by a generally stronger artistic climate in Rome and, of course, Florence. After going through his apprenticeship in Perugia, Raffaello was commissioned to work on the *Coronation of the Virgin* in the church of San Francesco. It was there that Raffaello was taken under the wing of another important master painter of the Renaissance, Pietro Perugino. Perugino inspired him and magisterially succeeded in influencing Raffaello's technique and style, something which is highly recognisable in Raffaello's first important painting, *The Marriage of the Virgin*, particularly when it comes to the specific stress given to the perspective and a certain delicacy when it comes to its figures. Despite this, Raffaello is remembered for taking Perugino's style and work and bringing it to another level, a more refined, polished one.

When he moved to Florence, Raffaello was a young man who was ready to be inspired by the Renaissance and by his masters. According to Vasari, he studied the works of Leonardo, Michelangelo and Fra Bartolomeo, and he also paid particular attention to Masaccio, whose style was much closer to naturalism and represented an artistic bridge between the Gothic period and the Renaissance.

Despite this, Raffaello was particularly influenced by both Leonardo and Michelangelo, particularly when it came to Leonardo and his style. He recognised the incredible advancements of Leonardo's painting technique and he was particularly inspired by Leonardo in producing a series of Madonnas including the *Madonna of the Goldfinch*, the *Madonna del Prato*, the *Esterházy Madonna* and *La Belle Jardinière*; he was also particularly influenced by Leonardo's *Madonna and Child* and drew inspiration from Leonardo's pyramidal compositions, as he was particularly taken by Leonardo's capability to group figures in a single unit while giving each of them a certain and a different personality.

Raffaello also used the lighting techniques conceived by Leonardo, particularly the sfumato. Much like he had done with Perugino, Raffaello managed to take Leonardo's technique to a whole different level by experimenting with gentler face traits in his paintings, which many have defined as sublime. Michelangelo was also a big inspiration for Raffaello, something which can be seen in *The Deposition of Christ*, particularly when it comes to human anatomy. Despite being deeply influenced by both Leonardo and Michelangelo, Raffaello was famous for moving away from both painters by creating a more luminous artistic style and ending up becoming a favourite with several patrons.

It was in Rome that Raffaello found his glory when, at the suggestion of Bramante, he started to work on the rooms in the Vatican papal apartments where he was commissioned to paint a number of frescoes; these rooms are the Stanza Della Segnatura and Stanza d'Eliodoro, which were entirely decorated by Raffaello himself; the other rooms, the Stanza dell'Incendio, were decorated by Raffaello and his assistants.

Raffaello also distinguished himself for being passionate about archaeology and ancient Greco-Roman sculpture, something which is also recognisable in his paintings.

This passion also had an effect on his work when in 1515 Leo X put him in charge of the preservation of marbles with Latin inscriptions, and in 1517 he was also appointed commissioner of antiquities for the city of Rome, something that led him to work on an archaeological map of the city.

He was also in charge of the papacy's different projects including those involving architecture, paintings and decorations. The last of Raffaello's works, the *Transfiguration*, was commissioned by Giulio Cardinal de' Medici in 1517 and is an altarpiece left incomplete and finished later by Raffaello's assistant, Giulio Romano. A complex work, the *Transfiguration* is elegant, polished yet often defined as being dramatic for its depiction of the crowded groups of figures which echo an early representation of baroque.

Raffaello died when he was only 37. His body was buried in the Pantheon in Rome, and he is often remembered as the Church's favourite painter.

Leonardo and Donatello

Another artist who is often associated with Leonardo, Michelangelo and Raffaello is Donatello. Donatello, who cannot be considered a competitor of Leonardo, as the two were not exactly contemporaries, is still one of the most interesting personalities in Renaissance culture and the artistic panorama of the time.

Born Donato di Niccolò di Petto Bardi and widely known by his peers and later by everyone else as Donatello, he was a sculptor who rose to fame during the Renaissance.

Unlike Leonardo, he was the son of a member of the Florentine Wool Combers Guild and had the chance to grow up at the home of the Martelli family, an important family in Florence connected to the Medici. It was during this time that Donatello learnt metallurgy and received training from a local goldsmith. When it came to his masters, the most important Donatello ever had was Lorenzo Ghiberti; it was he Donatello worked for when Ghiberti went on to receive the biggest commission of his life, the bronze doors for the Baptistry of the Florence Cathedral. Ghiberti managed to beat his rival Brunelleschi to the commission.

Despite this, Donatello learnt from Brunelleschi as well when the two travelled to Rome to study classical art, something that gave Donatello a strong understanding when it came to classical forms; connecting with Brunelleschi and spending time with him in Rome also gave him the chance to be influenced by his Gothic style, something which is incredibly present in Donatello's early works including *David*. This marble sculpture, famous for its delicate lines and almost expressionless face, has been judged perfect but not emotionally moving enough by many researchers; this was something that Donatello developed only later in his career when his works acquired a more dramatic and emotional element showing with notable precision different emotions including joy and sorrow. Donatello also worked with Michelozzo, another artist, on a regular basis on the production of different architectural tombs including the tomb of Antipope John XXIII and the tomb of Cardinal Brancacci.

Unlike Leonardo, Donatello was very close to the Medici family. It was Cosimo de' Medici who commissioned him to create the statue of *David*, and later on Donatello was even asked to complete a statue in bronze called *Gattamelata*, an equestrian monument dedicated to Renaissance leader Erasmo da Narni.

Much like Michelangelo, Donatello was often described as being difficult to deal with, and like both Michelangelo and Leonardo he never married.

Later on, Donatello completed a statue of *Magdalene Penitent*, commissioned by the convent at Santa Maria di Castello. His friendship with the Medici paid off in the long run and Donatello kept earning a retirement allowance to live off for the rest of his life. After dying of unknown causes in 1466, he was buried next to his favourite patron and friend Cosimo de' Medici.

Chapter 11

Leonardo and his Friends

Many things can be said about Leonardo, but that he did not like to connect with other people is not one of them. He was mostly a man who liked to spend time scrutinising others, often from a distance, as he was interested in understanding their secrets, their personalities, but he travelled, met people, sometimes princes, and spent his entire life forging precious relationships with many of them.

He was essentially a man who treasured people, who they were, and was interested in others, in learning about them, the more different the better. Leonardo was someone who celebrated conviviality, friendship and loyalty. He had charisma and boasted a reputation for being a positive force, exuberant in a way, happy, proactive with many different projects, and often the life and soul of the party or the court.

Naturally, he was also a man of contradictions. He was a scientist, an engineer, a mathematician in many ways, a scientific mind, and as such he would also take a step back and learn, really learn, from his surroundings, and from other people, sometimes from his own students, perhaps, who often served as models for his work.

He was a loyal man, someone who believed in friendship, he believed in being there for his friends, he was a generous man and was also found collaborating with some of his closest acquaintances and friends.

One of his most famous quotes about friendship is: 'Reprove your friend in secret and praise him in public', which proves the importance and the value that he placed on loyalty. Yet friendship to Leonardo was not just this; he was interested in people, he was a wonderfully curious person and it is in his constant search and thirst for knowledge that his acquaintances, his connections, his relationships and then, of course, his strong legacy were established, with the most important being the one established and later perpetrated by the group of the Leonardeschi.

A woman taking pictures of the Mona Lisa at the Louvre.

People taking pictures of the Mona Lisa.

Above: A mirror effect of the Mona Lisa.

Left: The Mona Lisa during COVID-19.

The Mona Lisa.

A pop art version of the Mona Lisa.

A statue of Leonardo da Vinci in Florence.

The Vitruvian Man
by Leonardo da
Vinci.

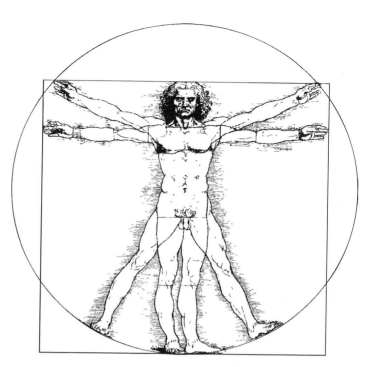

A statue of Leonardo da Vinci in Florence.

Two depictions of
Leonardo da Vinci.

Leonardo's flying machine (balloon).

Ginevra de Benci.

Scenes from *Io Leonardo* with Actor Luca Argentero directed by Jesus Garcés Lambert. Lucky Red Pictures: from the film *Io Leonardo* – a production by Sky and Progetto Immagine. (© foto Fabio Zayed e Maila Iacovelli)

Two depictions of The Last Supper.

The Leonardeschi

With the Leonardeschi we associate and define a group of Italian painters who were all taught or at some point in their life associated with Leonardo, who served as their friend and master. These people had the extraordinary opportunity to learn from the Italian genius of the Renaissance, succeeding in producing an extraordinary array of works which, often, were so similar to the ones Leonardo had been painting, mirroring his style so closely, that it was difficult, sometimes even impossible, for historians and curators to establish their authorship. Also, being a large group of students who had found in Leonardo someone who would inspire their work and strongly influence their style, it became extremely difficult for researchers and curators to differentiate between them all. This is, for example, the case for one of Francesco Melzi's painting, *The Flora*, which was first attributed to other students of Leonardo's from the same group before being finally attributed to him.

The group of the Leonardeschi featured different students who all worked, studied or were influenced by Leonardo in one way or another and this included some interesting names of the time including Giovanni Antonio Boltraffio, Marco d'Oggiono, Giampietrino Bernardino Luini, and Martino Piazza. Leonardo's favourite student and (many believe) lover Francesco Melzi is also often connected to the group of the Leonardeschi but he successfully established himself as a painter by his own talent and as an interesting character because of his role within the group and after Leonardo's death.

Much like the others, Melzi started at Leonardo's studio as his apprentice but because of the relationship he built with Leonardo, who trusted him more than anyone else, the several years he spent at his studio, and, nevertheless, their emotional and professional connection, he succeeded in developing a relationship with the maestro which went deeper and became more important than the one Leonardo ever established with anyone else. When it comes to the group of the Leonardeschi, it is interesting to note that all Leonardo's students managed to be influenced by him in one way or another, by adopting different techniques and styles developed by the Italian genius. These included the elegant style Leonardo used when painting facial traits, Leonardo's predilection for the sfumato, a technique he had created on his own, and, finally, Leonardo's partiality to nature and its beauties, plants and flowers, which turned into a proper fascination and study of botany, inspiring first himself and then his students.

Leonardo and Giovanni Antonio Boltraffio

Boltraffio was one of the first students to join Leonardo in Milan and even the first to be recorded in 1491 in one of Leonardo's notebooks, where he would make sure to note different aspects of his life from painting to expenses and daily errands and was recorded simply as Gian Antonio. Like those adopted by his peers, Boltraffio's painting style strongly reminds us of Leonardo's.

Despite his similarities with Leonardo, Boltraffio also enjoyed experimenting with different techniques, particularly focusing on the style and the concept behind his works. Later on, he was also deeply influenced by other painters including Bramantino and Andrea Solario. Boltraffio produced different paintings such as the *Resurrection of Christ*. Born into an aristocratic family, Boltraffio did not lack means and later achieved independence from Leonardo and his studio and decided to establish his own studio in 1498, where he started to produce portraits – something he excelled at, altarpieces and small paintings.

Leonardo and Marco d'Oggiono

D'Oggiono, who was recorded by Leonardo in his notes as just Marco in 1490, was one of the students whose style and technique more closely matched Leonardo's. As a consequence of this, he was strongly influenced by the Renaissance genius, as shown by several authenticated works which were finally attributed to him. D'Oggiono succeeded in learning Leonardo's techniques as well as adopting themes which were similar to Leonardo's, and this made it difficult for his work to be attributed to him. D'Oggiono was the son of a very successful goldsmith and, after training with Leonardo and starting a few collaborations with some of his students, he established himself as an independent painter and produced a vast selection of works with a religious theme including church altarpieces. He travelled extensively and also made copies of some of Leonardo's most famous works including *Virgin and Child*, *Virgin of the Rock*, and *The Last Supper*, something he created for a monastery in Milan. He died shortly after contracting the plague in 1524.

Bernardino Luini

Luini was born in Milan in 1485 and was not only influenced by Leonardo, with whom he worked as a young apprentice, but also by other masters living in Lombardy at the time. These painters had the merit of influencing and enriching his style in their own way. These artists included Bramantino who had been a big influence on Boltraffio's work, and Bernardino Zenale. Luini was particularly well known for having a strong predilection for painting frescoes with strong mythological and religious themes, something that deeply influenced his paintings, as they all seem to have a religious theme. When it comes to his relationship with Leonardo, Luini has been found to have been particularly influenced by Leonardo between 1506 and 1522. It was during this time that he completed some of his best works; these share some similar traits with Leonardo's works, and include his most famous work, the *Holy Family*. In this particular painting, Luini paid careful attention to the expressions and faces of his subjects, something Leonardo had done and explored all his life as he was always interested in human beings and the way they expressed emotions. Some of Luini's most interesting frescoes are *Story of Europa*, *Story of Cephalus and Procris* and the *Story of Mose*.

Leonardo and Martino Piazza

Martino, whose original full name was Martino de' Toccagni, was best known by only his surname, Piazza. Much like his contemporaries and members of the Leonardeschi, he had a predilection for the religious theme, something which he explored and fully represented in his works.

Piazza's collection included one work produced in partnership with his brother Albertino and three paintings which featured another important biblical figure, *Saint John the Baptist in the Desert*.

Leonardo and Giampietrino

Giovanni Pietro Rizzoli, best known as Giampietrino, was strongly influenced by Leonardo and many historians believe him to have been an official member of his studio since the very beginning, maybe from the mid-1490s, the time when Leonardo finally decided to leave Verrocchio behind and start his own studio. Giampietrino is one of the first names registered in the Codex Atlanticus.

Some of Giampietrino's paintings included a copy of *The Last Supper*, a painting which did not only have an impact on Leonardo but also on his students as well.

Leonardo and Bramante

The relationship Leonardo managed to build with his friends was completely different to the one he had perhaps with his apprentices. If he felt it was his duty to inspire, motivate and in a way give direction to his students, he was himself looking to be inspired, motivated and perhaps given direction in his relationships with his friends, and that is how he established a range of connections that just added to his persona and character.

Bramante is another interesting personality who populated Leonardo's universe. Donato Bramante's family were farmers who pushed him to study painting as well as the abacus; for everything else, he did not receive a traditional education, and much like Leonardo he did not study Latin and Greek. There are few details available concerning his first years of childhood or until 1477, when he started his painting apprenticeship and worked as an assistant of artist Piero della Francesca in Urbino. Despite spending time with Piero and having a first taste of what working as a painter could mean, he did not show a preference for painting as such and not much is known about him until he found his true vocation, which turned out to be architecture. It is his love and predilection for architecture that would bring him to rebuild St Peter's Basilica, and work on the Tempietto in San Pietro and the Belvedere Court in the Vatican.

After working on different frescoes for the façade of the Palazzo del Podestà in Bergamo, he moved to Milan and, under Ludovico Sforza, he started to work as an architect on different projects including the church of Santa Maria in San Satiro, a church which has the merit of showing the different artists in Bramante's life and how they both influenced and inspired him; this included Alberti, Mantegna, Brunelleschi, and, of course, the Urbino school. During this period, he was also asked to work on the cathedral in Pavia, succeeding in executing both the crypt and the lower part of the building for the same project.

Leonardo and Bramante had a strong relationship, and they often collaborated. In 1490, both worked on the structural problems of the tiburio or crossing tower of the Cathedral of Milan; like Leonardo, Bramante was an active member at the Sforza court and he was involved in organising events and festivals on their behalf. He also kept working as a painter but the only painting attributed to him is *Christ at the Column* at the Abbey of Chiaravalle. In Milan, he was also responsible for the designs of the piazza in Vigevano and his covered passageway for the Castello Sforzesco. When Milan was occupied by the French in 1499, Bramante was in Rome already working directly with Pope Alexander VI on the project of the fountains of Piazza Maria in Trastevere. He also worked at the monastery and cloister of Santa Maria Della Pace. It is under Pope Julius II that Bramante worked on the designs of the Belvedere and, in 1505, he also planned the new Basilica of St Peter in Rome, his greatest work, while also taking care of different side projects and acting as a town planner for Julius II on a new city plan for Rome; town planning was another love and passion he shared with Leonardo.

Bramante was an original character and someone who would, much like Leonardo, try to experiment with different things. Following Julius II's death, Bramante maintained his position under Leo X and offered him a plan which could have prevented the flooding of the Tiber. He was also asked to work on the Cathedral of Foligno but he became too ill, couldn't accept the commission and died the following year in 1514.

Bramante was a joyous individual, full of life, who had an aptitude for anything that was artistic: he was a painter, an architect and a writer, particularly interested in writing sonnets and with a fascination for Dante. With Leonardo, he had in common a strong thirst for experimentation and knowledge. He was a man of multiple talents and, much like Leonardo, he would never be found shying away from new projects or embarking on new, exciting adventures.

Bramante was also an individual with humour and wit, someone who would not take life too seriously but who also, equally, possessed a strong religious doctrine.

Unlike Leonardo's, Bramante's written works have not been found, and the only example of written work which carries his name is the one regarding the tiburio and its issues. Unfortunately, none of his sonnets has made it to us; Bramante wrote about twenty sonnets on different themes from love to comedy and religion. Sometimes he also showed a predilection for a somewhat crude style, perhaps more realistic than what people were used to at the time.

He was a man who liked to make fun of others but mostly of himself. Irony was something that was often present in his writing and irony was something else he shared with Leonardo; no wonder the two were friends. Leonardo himself was known for his personality, perhaps sarcastic at times, and he could often be found making fun of people, particularly of the people in his life.

It is no surprise that Bramante and Leonardo succeeded in connecting; they were two talented individuals who would thrive off each other's artistry but, above all, they were both incredibly smart men who had not been given the chance to study like others but managed to learn everything they needed to learn – experimenting with their work, opening their minds to new opportunities, ignoring their background, where they were from, focusing on what they could do with what they had, learning from their mistakes, improving themselves and expanding their horizons and those of the people they connected with.

Leonardo and Machiavelli

Many people connected with Leonardo, often after working together for the same patron or by collaborating together on the same project. It was a world in which people often worked together side by side for days, sometimes for years, with the result of inspiring each other in many ways. One of these intellectuals was Niccolò Machiavelli.

Machiavelli was born on 3 May 1469. His family was a family of means, where he had the chance to explore his love for books and politics, a passion which became his raison d'être for his entire life. He grew up in the Santo Spirit district of Florence and had two sisters, Primavera and Margherita. His mother was Bartolomea di Stefano Nelli and his father was Bernardo, a doctor who nurtured a passion for Cicero and his works. Machiavelli was deeply affected by the culture he breathed in his own house, and while it is not certain whether he was familiar with Greek, it is certain that he read the works of several Greek authors including Aristotle, Polybius, Plutarch and Ptolemy. He was also partial to Latin authors including Plautus, Terence, Caesar, Cicero, Sallust, Virgil, Lucretius, Tibullus, Ovid, Seneca, Tacitus, Priscian, Macrobius and Livy, and he also loved Italian authors; among his favourites were Dante and Petrarch.

Machiavelli's career in politics started following the conspiracy of the Pazzi, the plot to overturn the Medici family in Florence, something that followed several changes, particularly from a political point of view, in Florence. Changes that started dramatically with Italian Dominican friar and preacher Savonarola being burned at the stake following his attempt at denouncing corruption in Florence.

After Savonarola's death, Machiavelli was appointed to serve under Marcello Virgilio Adriani, Savonarola's successor, as Head of the Second Chancery. Despite being very young, only 29, and lacking any sort of practical political experience, he found himself covering a role of importance, something that deeply affected his life and passion for politics. It was experiencing politics and life as a politician for the very first time that first gave him the inspiration he needed to write books including *The Prince* and the *Discourses on Livy* which were published after his death. Later, Machiavelli was also appointed as Secretary to the Ten which was a committee that specialised in war affairs.

Without a doubt, Machiavelli deeply affected Florence's political life, and following his political appointment he was also asked on several occasions to go on different diplomatic trips including visiting Countess Caterina Sforza in Forlì. His diplomatic trips even took him overseas; he spent several months in France at the French court and he made the acquaintance of Georges d'Amboise, the cardinal of Rouen. Once his political career was finally sorted, he then decided to get married to Marietta di Ludovico Corsini, a woman who gave him six children (Bernardo, Baccina, Ludovico, Piero, Guido and Totto), one of whom died at birth, and who was considered a sweet woman who was selfless and understanding. However, Machiavelli's name was also famously associated with several other women including a courtesan who was well known in Florence with the name of La Riccia (which means 'the curly one' in Italian) and singer Barbera Salutati.

In 1502, Florence went through some important reforms which placed Piero Soderini as gonfaloniere (which meant he was in charge of the city) for life; previously gonfalonieri would only cover the position on a short-term basis which usually lasted for only two months. It was Soderini who decided to ask Machiavelli to create a Florentine militia, something which would have protected the Florentines in case of war; following this creation, Machiavelli then became chancellor of the newly created committee related to the militia.

Machiavelli and Leonardo collaborated on several occasions and on different projects. One of the most interesting was their first try at connecting the Arno river to the sea, something that would have both helped with the irrigation of the Arno valley and limited the water supply to the nearest city to Florence, Pisa, in case of war. With the Medici coming back to power in Florence, Machiavelli was imprisoned for over twenty days and accused of being anti-Medici. However, later on, his reputation was restored thanks to some of his friends and he was sent on some short diplomatic trips which impressed the Florentine family and granted him a bit more favour at their court. This was the moment which would change Machiavelli and his entire life; with his reputation compromised, he started to write and give full expression to his philosophical thought. In 1520, he published *The Art of War*.

The most fascinating, interesting and in many ways still relevant thing about Machiavelli was his set of ideas and philosophy which involved and affected different sectors. He was a philosopher, someone who much like Leonardo was not scared to question things. In his own words, Machiavelli said that it was 'good to reason about everything'. In *The Prince*, he also suggests that the prince himself should be a big questioner and listen patiently to the truth. Machiavelli also talks profusely about the notion of virtue as something that is an active power and can be achieved with self-discipline and self-knowledge, something even Leonardo was passionate about.

By the time Leonardo and Machiavelli met, they were respectively 51 and 34. The first was a great artist, Florence's number one man, who had painted *The Last Supper* already; the second was working for the government and still not one of the greatest philosophers of his time. Many are the researchers who have explored the relationship between the two. A few argue that they met briefly in Florence once but, according to Masters (author of *Machiavelli, Leonardo and the Science of Power*), they finally met after Machiavelli helped Leonardo get a commission to paint a mural. According to Masters, the two met during the war between Pisa and Florence and by working together on the diversion of the Arno experiment they planned to cut Pisa's water supply off. At the time of their meeting, they were both working at Palazzo Signoria, where Leonardo was planning his ultimately unfinished painting of *The Battle of Anghiari*. They both worked on the project of the diversion of the Arno, something which in perfect Leonardo style was never achieved; however, Masters argues that Machiavelli was so completely taken by the project that he wrote up to ninety-three letters concerning the excavation of the river bed.

Always, according to Masters, Leonardo's influence on Machiavelli was important, as shown by several similarities between Leonardo's notebooks and Machiavelli's writings; these include Leonardo's drawing of a military vehicle which again was never built but which had the merit of inspiring Machiavelli and his works.

There are several parallels between Leonardo and Machiavelli, which go from the way they thought and conceived life to their own writing. In his works, Machiavelli always tells his readers to never forget about war, not just during war itself but, particularly and especially, in times of peace. He goes further to admit that a wise prince should always be aware of war and its dangers; he needs to be the leader who is so wise and smart that he can anticipate war so that he can sense when his fortune is about to change. Leonardo's relationship with war is ambivalent; he was not involved directly in planning and scheming wars but he was someone who would plan some horrific war machines just to please his princes, the patrons he worked with. Following his time with Cesare Borgia, he would finally make the decision to profess himself ineluctably against any form of war, which he thought was bestial. Similarities can also be found in their approach to philosophy, particularly regarding the concept of virtue. When it comes to talking about virtue, Machiavelli, perhaps for the first time, introduces the concept of 'virtue' as just another way to turn a disadvantage into an advantage; according to Machiavelli, it is never enough to recognise one's limits but there must be some level of continuous work done to surpass them; once again, much like his thoughts and beliefs about war, good fortune is unpredictable and tables can turn in a second. Everyone should be prepared for life and its unpredictable nature.

In many ways, Leonardo's philosophy could be associated with Machiavelli as he did believe in working hard in order to turn disadvantages into advantages; he, after all, managed to turn the absence of a classical education, an obvious disadvantage, into a powerful advantage, a continuous thirst for knowledge which led him to discoveries and researches that covered different sectors.

Machiavelli died aged 58. His tombstone in Latin read 'Tanto Nomini Nullum Par Elogium' which means loosely 'such a great name, no adequate praise'.

Leonardo and Vasari

Some researchers believe that the two never met, yet no one ever talked about Leonardo the way Giorgio Vasari did. Italian painter, architect and the father of the history of art, without whom we would not know the stories of some of the most important men in the history of the art of our time, Vasari had a deep impact on Leonardo's story, giving us a very first glimpse of who Leonardo was and even what he looked like.

Vasari has been often described as a great student and a strong admirer of Michelangelo, without letting his admiration get in the way of his objectivity when it came to Leonardo, who, as we know by now, was not Michelangelo's biggest fan. Yet Vasari could not help but adore Leonardo, giving an almost impeccable description of his life.

Vasari trained with painter and glass artist Guglielmo de Marcillat, but he also took further training in Florence, where he worked directly under the patronage of the Medici while also having the chance to train with Florence painter Andrea del Sarto. Vasari distinguished himself as a biographer of the illustrious men of the Renaissance, and also worked as a painter, but was never widely appreciated for his techniques, which were criticised by different historians for being superficial and for the absence of a distinguishable trait. Vasari also worked as an architect and built the Uffizi in Florence; as mentioned he was far more widely appreciated for his book *Le vite de' più eccellenti architetti, pittori, et scultori italiani* (*Lives of the Most Eminent Painters, Sculptors, and Architects*) which he dedicated to Cosimo de' Medici, and which to this day is a perfect summary of some of the most interesting artists of all time.

Vasari and *The Battle of Anghiari*

There is always a constant, almost-supernatural interpretation of Leonardo, his universe and his works; maybe it was because of his extraordinary talent or his advanced intelligence. He was a man of many interests and yet so many mysteries, often fuelled by others, who, much like Vasari, would sing his praises and protect his work. A recent episode has seen Vasari at the centre of an interesting discovery which could confirm that Leonardo's *The Battle of Anghiari* is hidden behind one of Vasari's most famous works, *The Battle of Marciano* in the Chiana Valley.

Researchers have suggested that Leonardo's painting, of which we only have a few notes and sketches proving its existence, is hidden behind Vasari's painting. A clue to this is believed to be revealed in one of the painting's war banners which says 'Cerca Trova' which in English means 'Seek and you will find'.

This could confirm a major theory about Leonardo's masterpiece, believed to be three times bigger than *The Last Supper*, which argues that *The Battle of Anghiari* was never really lost but just protected by Vasari.

The Battle of Anghiari would have celebrated Florence's proclamation as a republic following the departure of the Medici family in 1503. Much like many of Leonardo's works, it was never finished, and when the family returned to power in 1560 it was covered by Vasari who had been asked to create a new painting on the exact same spot; it is interesting to note that Vasari chose a battle to paint as well, almost as if he wanted to perfectly hide and preserve (a cavity has also been found between the two potential paintings so that they don't touch and that must have avoided the erosion of the second painting) Leonardo's work.

Leonardo and Botticelli

Leonardo and Sandro Botticelli had the fortune of working with the same maestro as they were both employed at Verrocchio's studio.

The two were never competitors but friends, something which was quite odd for the time as they were both sought-after artists, but they did find a way to make their friendship work, inspiring each other and feeding off each other's artistry.

The friendship of Leonardo and Sandro Botticelli began when they were both students at Verrocchio's studio, where they met and worked together for a while; their friendship also had the chance to flourish further when they both worked as waiters in an inn which was not far from Ponte Vecchio. Later on, they also went and opened an inn together called Tre Rane (Three Frogs) which offered exclusive menus created by both artists, something that led Leonardo to explore his love for coming up with different recipes and even cooking; Leonardo got so involved in the project that he also started to conceive of time-saving cooking tools.

Alessandro di Mariano Filipepi, better known as Sandro Botticelli, was one of the most interesting painters of the Renaissance. His father, a tanner, tried to get Sandro to become a goldsmith but he was much more interested in painting and, under painter Filippo Lippi, he started his first apprenticeship. He also worked on his sculptural skills with sculptors and painters Antonio Pollaiuolo and Andrea del Verrocchio. Later, he even managed to establish himself as an independent artist.

Much like Leonardo and other painters and artists of the time, Botticelli embraced different styles and media forms when it came to art; within the religious theme, this included the altarpieces of *The Adoration of the Magi* and his input on part of the decorations of the Sistine Chapel. His work as part of the Sistine Chapel involved 'Stories of Jesus' which included 'The Temptation of Christ' for the chapel's northern wall and 'The Trials of Moses and Punishment of the Rebels' for the 'Stories of Moses' on the southern wall.

Like Leonardo, he worked for the Medici family and soon gathered a strong reputation, particularly for his portraits, which included one of Giuliano and later of Cosimo and Piero Medici.

Botticelli had a strong predilection for painting mythological scenes, going from romantic to promoting virtuous figures; he was a humanist and a perfect expression of a Renaissance man. These include some of his most loved works of art, *Primavera* and *The Birth of Venus*.

Leonardo in his own words and letters

Leonardo was a man who was not prone to sharing his sentiments, or to talking about his personal feelings or feelings in general.

Not even his friends really ever fully understood Leonardo, with his students and his lovers perhaps developing a marginal understanding of his persona. Everyone saw him the way others did, accepted his appearance of an unpredictable genius, but no one bothered to try to go below the surface.

Leonardo was a shy individual, a loyal one and someone who could be defined as a modern self-employed freelancer. His personality, or at least elements of it, succeeded in shining through in his own personal letters. It is in his letters that Leonardo, perhaps the real Leonardo, can really be found; it's in his condition under patronage having to deal with different patrons, searching for financial help, it's in the way he managed his group of students and apprentices and those who worked for him, it's in the polite way that he talked to his father, despite everything, despite their challenging relationship, that we can get a glimpse of who the real Leonardo was.

Leonardo had accurate but emotional penmanship, but if in his Codices he succeeded in being detached and perhaps cold, it's in his letters that his personality really succeeds in coming forward. The image we get is one of a Leonardo who is often concerned about money, and of a Leonardo who strongly believes in a fair and just system. It is also apparent that he held onto grudges, those he had for his brothers, and perhaps even subtly for his father, despite trying hard to show everyone, even himself, the opposite. He was also an affectionate, caring individual and proved his affection, loyalty and consistency as an individual and as a professional to countless friends and collaborators.

He was also in much need of approval; he wanted to be liked, never to a point that jeopardised his integrity or independence but just enough to feel part of something. Following the Saltarelli affair, Leonardo would probably seek his family's but mostly his father's approval for the rest of his life.

Leonardo did not only leave a vast amount of notes regarding inventions, ideas and life, he also equally left behind a number of letters that give us a little more information regarding Leonardo and the way he approached people, work, philosophy and even daily problems. Sometimes these letters offer us meticulous details about his approach and his work ethic, sometimes you can read his justifications as he tries to explain why he hasn't completed a project, why he has left everything behind and run after something else.

After reading his letters, the impression which comes through is one of a Leonardo who was often prone to a deep sense of inadequacy towards his family and patrons, yet of a Leonardo who was not afraid of defending himself and who had a strong understanding when it came to justice.

Leonardo's letters to his father

Leonardo's relationship with his father was extremely challenging. He felt abandoned and not really taken care of by him. Piero went and fathered other children, while Leonardo was always treated like the illegitimate son of the da Vinci family – he had no rights over the inheritance.

It is interesting to note, and no doubt a result of the culture of the time, how caring and polite Leonardo was when writing to his father. In one of the letters to him, he expressed what sounds like genuine pleasure at hearing about Piero's good health, as well as sorrow for hearing about Piero experiencing some past discomfort.

Leonardo's letter to his brother

Leonardo had a strained relationship with his siblings, guilty of having denied him anything from their father's will and wanting to deprive him of his inheritance from Uncle Francesco; the only one who loved him enough to leave him everything he possessed. Francesco was motivated by the need to repay Leonardo, who had helped him financially with some improvement works at his own house, while also trying to compensate for the obvious absence of Piero, who had failed to recognise Leonardo even before dying. In a letter that is believed to be addressed to his brother Domenico, Leonardo congratulates him on the birth of a child, poking subtle fun at his brother and reprimanding him for his absence of prudence.

Leonardo's letters to Sforza

Leonardo's letters to Sforza are still a perfect expression of Leonardo's condition as a Renaissance man who would have to provide services to a wealthy patron in order to survive; a condition which can be seen and analysed in his first letter, where he lists all the things he can do for Sforza and his house, which constitutes today the first prototype of a Renaissance CV.

Leonardo's letters to Lord Ippolito

It was the will, the litigation with his brothers that had a strong impact on Leonardo and brought him to ask for help anywhere he could find. He would ask important people including Lord Ippolito, who was Cardinal of Este, to intervene on his behalf and bring the litigation and the whole matter, which according to Leonardo's letters had been dragging for the past three years, to a favourable end for him. He just wanted to move on with his life and finally obtain what was his, what had been left to him by Francesco; he didn't want anything else but what was rightfully his.

Leonardo's letters to the Governor of Milan

The relationship with his brothers had some important effects on Leonardo and his life. Even in his letter to the Governor of Milan, he brings the subject of the litigation up as some sort of justification. In this polite, important letter, Leonardo tries to reassure the governor that they will meet again at Easter and that he will bring with him two paintings of the Madonna of different sizes which he hopes the governor will like. Again, he wonders whether the governor is angry at him as he hasn't received any response from him despite the numerous letters he has sent, and he just repeats that he wants to know whether he will still receive a salary and even enquires about the possibility of being lodged.

Leonardo's letters to Francesco Melzi

Leonardo was a humorous man, and that can easily be seen in his letters. He also loved his friends and collaborators alike dearly. Melzi, an alleged lover of Leonardo, was one of them, many believe his favourite, and in one of his letters to him Leonardo can be seen protesting, not so subtly, about Melzi not writing to Leonardo, or perhaps not writing enough.

He is, according to Leonardo, ignoring his incessant, continuous letters. Leonardo reproaches him sweetly and writes to him that when they meet again, he will make him write so much that he will no doubt become sick of it.

Leonardo's letters to Giuliano de' Medici

During his time in Rome, Leonardo worked for Giuliano de' Medici and it is in this letter, after the formalities, where he expresses himself so happy about Giuliano feeling so much better that he feels much better himself, that he admits how sorry he is that he couldn't complete a project for Giuliano. Leonardo blamed someone who had deceived him, someone who was paid before the time, before delivering the project, something Leonardo has no doubt he will deny, leaving Leonardo without finishing the work he paid for.

Leonardo also goes to comment about the fact that he had left nothing undone, he had been careful with this person, almost trying to justify things to himself about not finishing the project. Even at the end of the letter, he repeats how sorry he is that he has not been able to satisfy Giuliano's desire and that he can only wish he feels much better soon.

This letter stands as a clear justification for Leonardo's work. Leonardo felt constantly guilty about leaving entire projects unfinished and worried about the consequences of his actions. In this particular letter, he is evidently concerned he would lose his patronage and Giuliano's favour.

Chapter 12

Leonardo, the End

The veins, the muscles, the beauty of the human body, the anatomy depicted by someone who was an habitué of local morgues, someone who would spend time looking at cadavers, analysing them, learning about the extraordinary machine that is the human body. He knew so much about life that one cannot help but wonder what he thought about death.

By looking at Leonardo's *Vitruvian Man*, we can see that he did question death, he must have, no one portrays life like that, without ever stopping to question what happens when everything is brought to a halt and ends – so often – abruptly.

When it came to talking about death, he was famous for saying, 'Our life is made by the death of others. While I thought that I was learning how to live, I have been learning how to die. As a well-spent day brings happy sleep, so life well used brings happy death.' It would be interesting to understand what he thought about his life, whether he thought he had spent it well and whether he was going to have, in his own words, a 'happy death'. As usual, Leonardo did not express his opinion, did not leave his thoughts behind on whether he had spent a good, happy life and whether he deserved in his own words to have a happy death.

He had a full life, he was a man of many interests and had the ability to change his path when he felt it was not going the way he wanted it to; even the last years of his life were not exactly quiet and, before moving to the last phase, he went through different changes.

In 1512, for example, while in Milan he found himself having to stop his works and efforts for the creation of an equestrian monument for Italian aristocrat Gian Giacomo Trivulzio; this was brought to a halt by the invasion of Swiss, Spanish and Venetian forces which drove the French away from Milan. Trivulzio, who had led the French forces during the invasion of Milan, had been the one to commission Leonardo to

105

create a magnificent monument consisting of a bronze horse and a rider imposing themselves on a marble framework. The monument would have had a double function, had it been completed: it would have not only been another magnificent work of art but would have also housed Trivulzio's sarcophagus. Leonardo produced several sketches, but the actual monument was never completed.

In 1513, Leonardo went to Rome and was received by Pope Leo X, son of Lorenzo, 'il Magnifico'.

A new but short phase in his life started and from 1513 to 1516, Leonardo decided to spend most of his time living in the Belvedere Courtyard, Villa Belvedere, in the Apostolic Palace. It was here in Rome that he had the chance to work side by side with his competitors Michelangelo and Raffaello.

Leo X distinguished himself for being an exceptional patron, with a strong love for the arts and the sciences alike. His influence and power in Rome represented a great opportunity for Leonardo. While in Rome, according to Vasari's notes, Leonardo received a monthly stipend in exchange for providing works of art. He quickly moved into the beautiful rooms, which had been specifically decorated for him, of Villa Belvedere and started a moderately peaceful patronage. He was not on his own but was granted a small group of collaborators to move in with him as well.

Leonardo loved Rome and living in Villa Belvedere. He particularly enjoyed exploring his interests when it came to botany, studying different plants for his works.

Even in Rome, despite being extraordinarily inspired by its beauty, its art, Leonardo was still not interested in working directly on his paintings; it was still the engineering, the more scientific work that was always more appealing to him, and that is how he got himself involved working on different projects including devising a plan to drain the Pontine Marshes.

During his time at the Villa Belvedere, he also continued his work of dissecting cadavers, hoping to find more valuable information on a treatment for vocal cords and hoping to regain the Pope's favour, although dissecting was not something which was condoned by the church.

However, as it turned out, not even Rome's beauty was enough to hold him down, to make him stay, to satisfy his needs and meet his expectations. Once again, despite his age, he was looking for something else.

Leonardo was starting to grow frustrated, not just because of the lack of finances that would support once and for all his dedicated studies and researches, but also because of a clear lack of motivation and perhaps jealousy. In Rome he did not feel very motivated, not even from an artistic point of view, he was not being as productive as other painters at the Villa Belvedere, with these being Raffaello and Michelangelo, and that somehow added to his annoyance.

Rome was incredibly competitive and he was not being commissioned enough, partly because Rome and the Medici were all almost obsessed with Raffaello, who was a favourite of the church and was working non-stop. Leonardo did not feel appreciated; he marvelled at Rome and its beauties, but really there was nothing for him there, and that is why he decided to take a step in a different direction.

The jealousy towards Raffaello and other painters and the lack of motivation had the predictable consequence of bringing Leonardo's experience, his journey with the Medici, to an end. Once again, it was time for him to find another patron.

When, in 1515, Milan was reconquered by the French, by King Francis I more specifically, Leonardo had another opportunity at patronage. King Francis, who had been a fan of Leonardo from the very beginning, asked him to come work for him. That is how Leonardo left his studio in the Belvedere and moved to France, where he was given the manor house Clos Lucé, near the King's residence at the royal Château d'Amboise, where he created plans for a big castle for the King in Romorantin and also designed and built a mechanical lion.

Clos Lucé had a fascinating history of its own, a wonderful structure next to the castle, and was famous for having once had among its guests the famous D'Artagnan, as he escorted Nicolas Fouquet, the superintendent of finance arrested at Nantes, who was accused of maladministration of the state's funds and harmful accusations at the expenses of the monarch.

Amboise was a town in central France's Loire Valley and was famous for its castle and for Château du Clos Lucé, which today houses a small museum which displays some of Leonardo's designs.

Bought by Charles VIII in 1490, the castle was originally built during the reign of Louis XI in the fifteenth century and turned later into a less formal residence for King Charles and his wife, Anne of Brittany. The king succeeded in changing the castle into an elegant Gothic palace.

He built two large cavalry towers, which allowed horses and carriages to go back and forth between the town and the château's terraces.

Later on, future King Francis I came to live to the castle with his sister Margaret of Navarre and his mother, Louise of Savoy. Francis became a patron of Leonardo in the last years of his life and legend says that he used to visit his old friend through an underground passage which connected the castle with Château of Amboise, Leonardo's home where he lived with Mathurine, his maid.

In France, under his new patronage, he was the first painter and engineer of the king and had the chance, once again, to bring over some of his famous pupils, Salai and Melzi, as well as some of his famous paintings including the *Mona Lisa* and *St John Baptist*. He was a favourite with the king who loved to come to visit him, many say, once a day and would not ask him for anything but the pleasure of his presence at court. The two developed a strong connection, a friendship that became extremely important to Leonardo, especially as he advanced in age.

According to different researchers, there is also a chance that Leonardo da Vinci even had the opportunity to spend some time with or at least meet Anne Boleyn, as she stayed at the court in France. Many argue that there's a chance that Anne might have even seen the *Mona Lisa* and met the maestro. It is fascinating to think about these two figures coming together, perhaps meeting for the first time; who knows what Leonardo thought of Anne, whether he saw in her what everyone else saw. Many also speculate about him taking her portrait, something that probably never happened. It is interesting to think that everything occurred while Leonardo was in France, later in his life, during the last part of his journey.

In France, Leonardo focused on other things rather than painting and that included projects in the fields of engineering and architecture and particularly the project of Romorantin which took a large part of his days. In the winter of 1517, he also produced a vast array of sketches which included designs for the castle, gardens and an intricate network of canals. Despite this, the castle was never completed but some elements of Leonardo's designs are believed to be traceable in other castles including Chambord and Blois. By keeping in line with the previous patronage, where he had been in charge of the events at the court, Leonardo also planned in 1518 the wedding festival of Lorenzo di Piero de' Medici and Madeleine de la Tour d'Auvergne at Amboise.

Leonardo's will was finished in 1519 after he started to deteriorate as a consequence of his poor health; legends, stories and several paintings and representations alike suggest he died in the arms of the French king, who loved him dearly.

As his health deteriorated, he was not alone; Melzi was there – Salai had left a long time ago – his cook stayed behind and so did his maid, they would not have left him for anything in the world, they were a unit, a family, connected by an indissoluble bond.

Eventually he became ill and took to his bed. He died at Clos Lucé on 2 May 1519 at the age of 67, with a stroke being the official cause of death.

He was buried at Saint-Florentin in Château d'Amboise. Not much is known about his remains as Saint-Florentin was damaged during the French Revolution and demolished by Napoleon I. His bones were found in 1863 but, with no real evidence that those remains were, in fact, Leonardo's, they were then moved to St Hubert Chapter, where they are still believed to be today, with a bust marking the exact spot.

After his death, his possessions were distributed between his best students and lovers. Melzi received a great collection, maybe the most important, of books, painting supplies and paintings; he was the one in charge of keeping Leonardo's memory alive, the one perhaps even Leonardo believed to be his best student, the artistry in him that kept living. Salai received a house in Milan with a garden; he was also the one to maintain possession of both the *Mona Lisa* and *St John the Baptist*, but it is unclear how he managed to do so. He sold the *Mona Lisa* to King Francis I.

As established years before, Leonardo's brothers received his land while his maid received a fur coat.

In his last days, Vasari describes a Leonardo who kept saying that he had offended God by failing to practise his art until the very end. Despite what he wrote, practising his art was, in fact, something that he managed to do until the end of his days despite suffering from a stroke that had paralysed his right hand. He was left-handed and kept writing until the end.

It is interesting, as per a documentary produced by Rai, that one of the last notes found in his notebooks is a simple passage abruptly interrupted. Leonardo was writing about geometry, something incredibly important that required his full attention, yet something else was also bothering him and interrupting his flow, his train of thought. Maybe supper was ready and his cook was calling him from the other room, trying to get him to leave his work, his writing, and come eat something. He worked too hard, his cook took care of him and would probably push him to rest, maybe she was getting impatient, and was now calling him with more vigour. It is interesting to note how Leonardo's passage about geometry ends with his final words being 'etc., etc., otherwise the soup will get cold'.

He died quietly, remembered, yes, but discreetly, not with much of a fanfare. He did right by his lovers, those who had been with him from the very beginning, and then he left. He was a man with no education, ginger, left-handed, and a bastard, he was also an engineer, a scientist, and, yes, even a painter. He started as a David, small, young, arrogant, but he died as a Goliath, a giant of immense knowledge, intellect and interest. Little did he know he would leave a world mourning for him, even centuries later.

Chapter 13

Leonardo, a Man of Mysteries

Leonardo da Vinci was a man of many mysteries. His brilliant mind was a matter of suspicion; no one had ever been that inquisitive when it came to his surroundings, the world, nature itself, people and friends. He was a man who would always look beyond reality and would spend his entire life and career searching for the truth of things. It is probably why he was not particularly interested in just producing aesthetically pleasing works of art; he would do intense, continuous research when it came to his work, and not necessarily just to reflect it on the canvas but to understand it so this research could potentially be of use to him or those after him.

A man so smart, so interesting and interested in everything that surrounded him was not someone who could be simply defined with just one label. He could hardly be confined in any box – he was a man who would strive to always push boundaries with his life, his paintings, his inventions and sometimes even his own ideas, generating incredible curiosity and being shrouded in a mysterious allure for centuries.

Many have been bold enough to attach to him different labels; some call him a member of the Order of the Knights Templar, others an alien or someone from the future, perhaps from our time, as they believe him to be so futuristic and innovative in his works that he couldn't possibly be just another Renaissance man; not that he ever was just that.

He was a man of mysteries, of messages, iconography and symbolism; often these mysteries involved and were attached to his works, his paintings, his own authorship and even his life.

Leonardo and the Templars

The figure of Leonardo has been given a number of labels. From wise old man to genius, scientist, engineer and painter, many have tried to fit him in a box. When this fails, they have also tried to give further explanations to his person, often attaching a mystical attribute to his personality that could magically explain why Leonardo was so advanced and such a pioneer in everything he did. This has had the merit of sanctifying his figure to iconic levels.

Many have made an attempt at explaining his being in books, movies and TV series, with the effect of him becoming more and more popular as a consequence of this.

A popular explanation and representation of Leonardo and his work, which has contributed to Leonardo's fascination and perhaps alleged mysticism, is the one found in *The Da Vinci Code*, a book, a movie and a gripping fictional story that has had the advantage of showing Leonardo as a revolutionary mind who saw the light and the truth before anyone else and decided to disseminate his ideas through his works of art.

In the movie and Dan Brown's book, Professor Robert Langdon (played by Tom Hanks) tries to unravel the truth, to solve a mystical puzzle centuries old, a quest which questions both Catholicism and Leonardo da Vinci's paintings. According to Dan Brown's fictional work, Mary Magdalene, a biblical prostitute – or that is what we have been led to believe her to be – was originally meant to play a different role in Catholicism and Jesus' life, and far from being just another woman saved by Jesus, she was the one he had originally intended to marry in order to start his church and build a more women-friendly, feminist if you like, church.

Before Dan Brown, *The Da Vinci Code*, and various online theories that have turned the historical, yet mysterious, figure of Leonardo into someone involved in matters of Holy Grails and Knights Templar, Giorgio Vasari, centuries before, in his biographical works, had already spoken incredibly highly of Leonardo.

Vasari almost considered Leonardo a divine creature, and according to many, the man, the inventor, who was so flawless in his beauty and grace, was also someone gifted with supernatural gifts, someone who had, indeed, perhaps, very little to do with our world. In many ways, Vasari was the first to attribute to Leonardo perfect qualities that made him a model when it came to the arts and the sciences.

We can see how the figure of Leonardo could be included in such a powerful, mystical narrative. Leonardo himself was a man who was extremely sensitive and who had a love for anything that was beautiful and delicate, yet he was also witty, intelligent and in many aspects too advanced for our world: proof could be found in his inventions but also in his curiosity, in his lack of fear for anything that he didn't know, for anything that was different or just that did not conform with the society of the time.

Rumours that Leonardo had been involved with the Knights Templar or that he had been a Templar Knight himself have raised eyebrows with several people, particularly historians and curators, questioning the veracity of these theories especially as they find very little confirmation in Leonardo's life, connections and world. Despite both the book and the movie always being promoted as a product of fiction, it has been interesting to see how little it took for Leonardo and his mysterious world to be connected to the mythical world of the Templars. This is something that he would probably have been enraged about as he was a man who would strive all his life to be considered as an engineer rather than a painter, a man of science, a practical man. By looking at his life and the choices he made, it would be natural to assume that he was not the kind of person who would decide to join a religious order of Templars.

Despite this, what has really troubled researchers and historians alike is that Leonardo's paintings have always been different to anyone else's, have always had a certain allure of mystery, particularly when it came to symbolism. Those same details, which some of us had missed before, remain a mystery and have been positioned in the spotlight ever since; in *The Last Supper*, these details include the incredibly feminine facial traits of one of the apostles, making a few people wonder if Leonardo had wanted to paint a woman instead.

Truth be told, Leonardo had a partiality to painting men with the most angelic features. He was a perfectionist, a man who was interested in people, he used to follow men in the street just to understand how to paint them, how to perfectly paint their expression, how to transfer seamlessly to canvas those traits only a human being could possess, and that is why he perhaps had decided to give such an angelic, delicate element to Jesus' apostles. Perhaps, from his perspective, he was directly reflecting Jesus' light by being so close to him. Leonardo's painting style was graceful and would often confer the same trait to his characters in his paintings.

Something that could also reject the Templar theory is Leonardo's strong personality. At this stage, it is interesting to note that Leonardo was not a man who would easily follow orders. Despite probably suffering from social anxiety and a sense of inadequacy, he was extremely strong-minded; he was a man who, despite being jovial and loved at court, preferred to be on his own, work on his own, and was always followed by a small group of his closest and dearest friends as he travelled for his work at the different courts in Italy and abroad. He was not easily manipulated, and he was so unpredictable in his ways, behaviour and personality that he had serious problems following others. Even under patronage, he was not easily persuaded to follow his patron's rules – he would often do what he wanted, with very little worry or care about consequences. He was not made to be a soldier and follow rules, perhaps not even for the greater good.

Yet he was mysterious and he did know more than other people in his circumstances; his studies proved a certain advancement when it came to developing scientific and engineering theories.

Books and movies have contributed to granting Leonardo once again a reputation for being a genius, someone ineffable, someone who was not fully understood at the time. Many judged him to be unpredictable and not structured enough when it came to his work; the mainstream media has helped him reach that level of fame and iconic status that has made him once again modern, relevant and on-trend, and by connecting his name to the Knights Templar, he has become once again a mythical creature with an allure of mystery.

But even if he had been involved with the Knights Templar, who were they and why would they have been interested in someone like Leonardo in the first place?

The Knights Templar were a large organisation which found its origins during the medieval era and focused on protecting those who travelled in the Holy Land as well as carrying out military operations. Their story was fascinating and mysterious and has inspired several writers in different fictional books.

It is interesting to note that originally, despite being an independent group, the Knights Templar even received a public endorsement from the Catholic church.

When in 1099, during the crusades, Christian armies captured Jerusalem, which had been until that time under Muslim control, many

Europeans started visiting the Holy Land, which had gained a reputation worldwide. These tourists began to be subjected to violence, which often included robbery and murder, as they inexpertly crossed different territories which were still under Muslim control.

Such violence at the expense of Catholic tourists led a French knight, Hugues de Payens, to start a military order created from his eight relatives and acquaintances; this order eventually found its headquarters in Jerusalem's Temple Mount; this group was originally called the Poor Fellow-Soldiers of Christ and the Temple of Solomon.

From 1139, the Knights Templar started to be involved in the society of the time and even obtained different benefits; these included an exemption from paying taxes and being under no one else's authority except the Pope's. That's how they succeeded in building a reputation and an influence, maintaining a strong level of financial independence.

It was not easy to be part of the order as its knights maintained a severe code of conduct which involved members swearing an oath of poverty, chastity and obedience. Knights couldn't drink or gamble and had to pray daily; they also distinguished themselves for their adoration of the Virgin Mary. The order also built several castles and won victories against Muslim armies; however, when these took control of Jerusalem in the late twelfth century, the Knights Templar had no other choice but to relocate somewhere else. By 1303, they had effectively founded a new headquarters in Paris.

During the same time, they were also persecuted and tortured for false charges including homosexuality, fraud, corruption and devil-worshipping, and shortly after, following pressure by other rulers on Pope Clement, the order was dissolved and their assets assigned to a rival order. Despite this, many believe that the Knights Templar order still lives underground today, particularly several other groups which started around the eighteenth century, and which shared the medieval knights' rituals and traditions. Several theories also believe that the Knights Templar have hidden and guarded the Shroud of Turin (linen believed to have been placed on Jesus Christ's body before burial) for centuries.

It was not easy to get involved in any military order and, according to Alan Forey in his book *Military Orders and Crusades*, when it came to the military order, entry was not open to everyone and there were several restrictions when it came to having access to membership, with one of these being exclusivity, as these particular religious groups were only reserved for free men, especially between the twelfth and thirteenth centuries.

Leonardo was a free man. He was also a revolutionary thinker and there is a chance that, far from being linked or connected to the Knights Templar, he was much more interested in people, his customers, his family and his friends. He had, after all, a different perspective on the world, a different point of view which took a step away from everything the Roman Catholic church and the religion of the time stood for. When working on his paintings, particularly focusing on the symbolism he often used in his art, there is a chance that Leonardo's main intention was not to give people a reason to link him to anything mysterious or mystical but mostly to give others a chance to venture out of the constraints created by the Roman Catholic church and explore for themselves what they wanted to believe in.

Whether or not he was involved in the Knights Templar, and with the legend becoming the myth itself, Leonardo did use his influence first and then his art as a way to channel his beliefs and disseminate his ideas, in a subtle way in order not to raise any suspicion with members of the Catholic church.

It is important to remember that at the time, during the Renaissance, the Catholic church had lost the influence it had boasted during the Middle Ages. It was a time when men felt like they had the right to question everything they had been taught and that included God – a detached, selfish god who had left them alone in the darkness of the Middle Ages for too long, forgetting about them, leaving them to suffer from pestilences, poverty and famine, a god that had done very little to improve their living conditions.

With the Renaissance being a much lighter, positive time, it was easy, a little too easy, for men to start questioning everything, basking in the light created by the endless possibilities the Renaissance period stood for, and finally knowing for sure that whatever they wanted to become, whatever they wanted to do or be was in their hands; they had finally found out they had power and that had nothing to do with some distant god.

During this time, and the flourishing of humanism, Leonardo started to become a figure of prominence and importance. He was influential;

several noblemen and families alike wanted to work with him despite his lack of structure and the fact that he did not seem inclined to finish any of his works. He built a reputation for being unreliable, yet he quickly became a genius, someone everyone wanted to be close to, someone everyone wanted to work with. He had the freedom of painting or working on everything he wanted, he could disseminate ideas but he was smart enough to know that if he wanted to start spreading different ideas, changing the world and giving his contribution, he needed to be careful, that he couldn't leave anything to chance, that as revolutionary as the Renaissance times were, and that people were finally shaking off the brutality and the poverty and the close-mindedness of the Middle Ages, he had to tread carefully with his ideas and with his inventions. He was a man of many mysteries, a man who wrote from right to left, leaving many wondering why; some seemed to believe that it was because he didn't want to smudge the ink, being left-handed, while others strongly believed that he didn't want the Catholic church to find out about his discoveries or perhaps messages, particularly as Leonardo was a pioneer in everything related to science, medicine and astronomy.

Leonardo, as seen by Freud

Many people have tried to explain Leonardo and his mysteries; some have particularly focused on his talent, sometimes on his beauty, often his life and then, of course, his sexuality.

Freud was one of these. He tried to understand Leonardo by studying him and trying to uncover his mysterious, beautiful mind. According to Freud, Leonardo, the man always associated with anything that was mysterious and mystical, was a creature of many contradictions.

He was sweet, kind and didn't like any antagonism (hence, probably, why he fled to France to avoid Michelangelo, or so rumours say), he was peaceful and didn't eat meat as he had too much respect for animals. He was also, as we know by now, fascinated by birds, and, according to Freud, he used to buy them at the market just for the pleasure of freeing them from their cage and studying them for his research. Yet, despite being a sweet man, and having such a kind disposition towards the world, Leonardo remained quite impartial and cold when it came to events surrounding his life and his world. He used to accompany criminals on their way to their executions just to study their facial features and sketch them in his notebooks. He also, as we know by now, used to come up with offensive weapons when he was working for Cesare Borgia. In many ways, not even Freud succeeded in understanding whether Leonardo was an artist with scientific interests or a scientist with an artistic disposition. He was detached, objective and most certainly looked at reality the way a scientist would, someone perhaps too practical to be involved in anything that wasn't what he could see, touch and study.

He was also described as not being very affectionate or having a predisposition to love; many researchers have been convinced that despite him being homosexual, and being surrounded by incredibly beautiful, handsome young men, some of these often posing as his models, he was not sexually active – most believe him to be celibate. Freud attributes the lack of passion in his life to his detachment – mental, emotional, and physical – from his mother. Love or hate was not something that was supposed to be felt or experienced but studied. According to Freud's notes, it is not that Leonardo, in his genius, didn't understand passion as something that could move and inspire everything else; he just preferred to question both love and hate and understand where both had originated from, why and with what effects.

Freud described a Leonardo detached from his maternal figure; he had grown up mostly on his own, immersed in nature, having no one to care for him but strong male figures including his grandfather, uncle and, consequently, although from afar, his father. It's this detachment, the absence of a strong maternal figure to care for him and protect him from the world that could explain, according to Freud, Leonardo's emotional detachment. Caterina, his mother, and Leonardo later in their lives managed to rekindle their relationship when Caterina went to live with her firstborn, falling ill shortly after. She was buried with a funeral which, according to Freud's notes, was extravagant and costly (according to other researchers, Leonardo spent the bare minimum for his mother's funeral and many historians have confirmed that he used to spend much more on clothes for himself and his models and friends).

Another passage that may explain Leonardo and how his mysterious mind worked can be found in his notebooks, in a passage where he talks about vultures and which Freud decided to single out from many others to explain Leonardo and the way he approached the world once more.

In this passage, Leonardo describes a memory from his past, something that allegedly happened when he was still in the cradle but that was so shocking that it deeply affected him even at such a young age; in the episode a vulture came down to him, opened his mouth with its tail and struck him several times with its tail against his lips.

In analysing this memory, Freud uses psychoanalysis, which he defined as being an excellent method to bring to light what this particular memory really conceals. The first thing Freud does is to quickly dismiss the idea of the memory being real; as much as he appreciates Leonardo and the nature of this memory for how different and 'out of this world' it is, he does not believe the memory to be legitimate but instead to constitute more of a hidden desire. Freud connects the dots, believing that the vulture episode was nothing more than an expression of Leonardo's sexuality and specifically homosexuality; the tail, or as Leonardo calls it, 'the coda', is nothing more, according to Freud, than the male organ and the act of the tale striking on his lips is a representation of fellatio.

Another explanation and theory, also by Freud, links once again back to his mother and associates the kisses of the vulture with a call for a different love, a maternal love, something Leonardo clearly missed for his entire life. It was his mother's lips that he missed, the ones he talked about in this crafted, fabricated memory of his, something that probably never happened but that still, according to Freud, has the potential to express both Leonardo's homosexuality and his feelings of neglect, abandonment and craving when it came to his mother, something that never really abandoned him and something that clearly had an impact on his life and art. In his notes, Freud believes that Leonardo had some unresolved issues towards his maternal figure and that Caterina, by being so distant and far away, living her life with another family, other children, became a prominent figure in Leonardo's universe.

However, later, researchers have established that vultures had been incorrectly translated from Italian to German and that Leonardo was talking about a kite.

Leonardo was a man of contradictions, a man of mysteries and perhaps even a man who fabricated memories in order to share what he really thought, his ideas, his stories, his secrets.

Leonardo and *The Virgin of the Rocks*

The *Mona Lisa* is not the only work by Leonardo to have become famous for its hidden meanings and mysteries; several more could be included in this list, and one in particular comes to mind: *The Virgin of the Rocks*.

Commissioned in 1483 by the Confraternity of the Immaculate Conception, this painting was originally intended as part of a large altarpiece for the church of San Francesco in Milan. In perfect Leonardo style, the painting was delivered late, not until 1508, and unfinished. This was not something new to Leonardo, yet it was something the confraternity was not too happy about, and which even today, centuries later, is still visible in the painting, with the angel's hand being sketched and not finished.

The delay, this time, was not completely Leonardo's fault. He took his time to deliver projects but, in this particular case, the main dispute was about money. Leonardo had been promised a set fee and a bonus at the painting's completion. However, as it turned out, the bonus was not incredibly generous and Leonardo, as an act of revenge, decided to sell the painting to a private seller (it now graces the Louvre museum). Later, he managed to find a solution with the confraternity and started to work on a second version of the same painting; this second version is today in the National Gallery. At the time, patronage, any type of patronage, was a challenging relationship, both for the artist and for the other party.

Despite this, *The Virgin of the Rocks* (both copies of the painting) is one of the best representations of Leonardo's symbolism.

There are several explanations behind the symbolism and the history of *The Virgin of the Rocks*. The story and the narrative are biblical and so are its characters, which include the Virgin, Christ, St John and an angel. However, despite this, the background of the painting is not what we would expect from such a biblical scene – it is not set in the desert but in a dark landscape with mountains, caves and water.

The story is not new, as many tales talk about a legendary meeting between Jesus and St John the Baptist when they were just babies. According to the legend, they met following King Herod's order of a massacre of the innocents; they escaped trying to save themselves, and it is at that time that the holy family fled to Egypt and met St John on their way.

Leonardo has the merit of showing the holy figures with the sfumato technique, almost seen as through smoke, which paints them in daylight and beautifully contrasts with the dark background. Leonardo is not trying to give his own interpretation of the biblical scene, he is bringing to the canvas a set of metaphors; he paints rocks and the cave for their sanctuary connotations, as often Mary and Joseph were associated with these natural elements; the flowers in the painting also have a meaning of purity and atonement while the palm leaves symbolise the Virgin Mary and victory.

Something that makes the painting even more mysterious is the hidden drawing found by curators who examined *The Virgin of the Rocks*. Using a technique called infrared reflectography, a team from Florence was able to locate an under-drawing of a preliminary sketch of the painting itself; it looks like Leonardo had started something else and then abandoned it for *The Virgin of the Rocks*. That is a completely plausible theory considering Leonardo's unpredictable nature; he was an eclectic man, someone who was often found starting something new before finishing what he was doing first.

Leonardo and the *Salvator Mundi*

Leonardo was not what we would call a prolific painter; he was not Michelangelo, he did not have the discipline or perhaps even the interest to work very hard on his art for a long time. He was also not particularly interested in working with patrons when it came to art, and that made it even more difficult to produce a vast array of paintings.

This makes it even more interesting to consider the fame and the interest generated by some of his most famous paintings including the *Salvator Mundi*. Featuring Jesus Christ, the Salvator, the saviour, as he makes the sign of the cross with his right hand and holds a transparent orb in his left hand, the *Salvator Mundi* is believed to have been originally commissioned by Louis XII of France and his wife, Anne of Brittany.

For many years, the *Salvator Mundi* was also believed to be a copy made by one of Leonardo's students and only recently has been attributed to Leonardo himself; many think that Leonardo's authorship can be found in the transparency of the orb. However, even today, many curators reject the attribution. According to many, the orb, considered by many to be a solid glass ball, does not magnify and invert the material behind it, a detail someone like Leonardo would have added, while others believe that this was exactly how Leonardo had intended to paint it in the first place.

In 2008, experts were called to look at the *Salvator Mundi* and establish its authenticity.

No arguments were made against Leonardo's lost work of art and the painting received its authentication. Unveiled in 2011 at the National Gallery, the painting was later auctioned and sold at Christie's for $450.3m (£342.1m).

Purchased for the Louvre Abu Dhabi, the painting's big unveiling in 2018 never happened, which fuelled rumours of the painting not being a real Leonardo.

Leonardo, a man from the future

Leonardo was a pioneer in many areas; experimenting was natural to him and it was not something he was scared of. He would create the most beautiful things out of long, often years-long studies and researches; he would never shy away from novelty, from anything that had not been tried before, in fact that had the power of igniting his fire even more.

Nothing he did was standard or conformed to what was expected of him, hence why he was never a favourite with patrons, managing, despite being financially dependent, to keep some level of independence when it came to his work.

He would lose himself so much in experimenting and always finding different ways to express himself creatively and scientifically that he would forget his works or what he was supposed to do instead; experimenting took time and that is probably why Leonardo had problems with deadlines, let alone finishing some of his works and inventions.

Despite working hard on war inventions, particularly under the patronage of Francesco Sforza, Leonardo worked even harder on researching for inventions that are still today so advanced as to be almost defined as pioneering.

Leonardo's inventions, ideas and research studies were futuristic for the time but always intended to make life easier for people and satisfy their needs. Some of his inventions, ideas or even sketches were not based on reliable findings, others were not practical and some of these famous experiments were probably never even tried by Leonardo himself. However, he left a selection of different ideas he had that have come to constitute the very first step in different modern disciplines and inventions (serving perhaps as rudimentary prototypes).

His advancement in any field was so interesting and of such quality and importance to fuel rumours which would depict Leonardo as a man who came from the future, someone who was too revolutionary for our world.

Submarines

When it came to submarines, it almost came naturally to him. Leonardo had the simple idea of designing ships that had the extraordinary ability to travel underwater. It was a meticulous engineering experiment that never saw the light of day, and was never started, let alone completed. Leonardo, particularly following his direct experiences with princes and war, was too scared of his sketches and inventions falling into the wrong hands and becoming another war tool at human beings' expense.

Helicopters

Leonardo was a man with a vision and his vision had wings. He wanted to fly, by looking at birds, their movement, and through his studies and researches he succeeded in developing an idea, among many others, for a man-powered helicopter, something which was eventually brought to completion by a team of inventors in 2013. Da Vinci's is considered one of the earliest helicopter prototypes.

Pigments

Perhaps it was not that he did not like to paint anymore; perhaps it was that painting did not give him the right inspiration. Experimenting with colours took time and different tests and Leonardo could just not work under pressure.

When it came to his art, Leonardo would always try to find something that would be both different and functional and that is exactly how he ended up experimenting with different techniques. And when it came to painting, he was always the one to try different techniques which included the sfumato, and he was also experimental when it came to the use of colours, especially moving away from the traditional colour techniques (pigment mixed with water and egg yolk) in favour of water and oil-based colours.

Fridges

Leonardo came up with a very first prototype of the fridge while working under the patronage of the Sforza. That was a moment in his life when he realised he could have been so much more than just another painter at court.

Parachutes

He was greatly fascinated by the idea of flying but he never tested a parachute. He most certainly played with the idea in his sketches, with his parachutes being made of sealed cloth held up by poles in wood. That is exactly how he succeeded in providing a very first prototype.

Human evolution

Leonardo's study of comparative anatomy brought him to closely research the relation of the two species and the similarities between men, apes and the like. Many have also argued that traces of Leonardo da Vinci's pioneering ideas, this time about geological evolution, can also be found in the two different paintings of *The Virgin of the Rocks*.

Sketching

According to different researchers, sketching was for Leonardo an important part of planning any painting in advance and perhaps seeing it on paper for the first time. He would usually sketch something before moving everything, his thoughts, ideas and his narrative to the actual painting. He was also famous for sketching ideas for his inventions and for almost absentmindedly drawing those who would populate his universe.

Storytelling and symbolism

Leonardo's paintings distinguished themselves for two important elements: storytelling and symbolism. He would often work on religious paintings, as per the Renaissance tradition, but he would add a different element to them, add to their stories by almost giving a different personality to his characters. Symbolism was also incredibly represented and important in all his works.

Sight

Sight and its study were present in several notebooks by Leonardo. He was particularly interested in the studies of optics while also researching different theories which related to shadows, light and colours. He was interested in finally understanding how sight worked. In order to do so, he dissected eyes and found that the eye was formed by two concentric spheres: the outer *albugineous sphere*, and the inner *vitreous* or *crystalline sphere*.

Opposite the pupil, Leonardo found out that there was an opening into the optic nerve which had the ability to send images to the imprensiva of the brain, an actual physical organ of perception, coined by Leonardo, which collected all sensory information.

Solar power

During his time under the patronage of the Vatican, Leonardo came up with the idea of 'burning mirrors'. In the Codex Arundel, there are more than 200 designs which talk about the subject, but it is during his time under the patronage of Giuliano de' Medici that he carefully listed and explained how to produce large concave mirrors, particularly finding a solution to avoid shading.

Calculator

Being an extraordinary scientific mind, Leonardo even came up with the first calculator, a complex mechanism which later was labelled as a ratio machine.

Telescope

In the Codex Leicester, Leonardo wrote a passage where he talks about creating eyeglasses to be able to see the moon more clearly and goes in detail about the thickness of the glass he would use. Leonardo never actually created the telescope but his sketches prove that he was on the right path.

Robots

Leonardo was even capable of creating a robot, a rudimental, mechanical one but the very first prototype we have of a robot which he called an armoured knight and was capable of waving, moving its head and closing its jaw.

Leonardo and religion

One of the most interesting aspects when it comes to Leonardo and his universe is the idea of religion; even today, many researchers still debate about Leonardo and whether he was a member of the Catholic church.

He had never been incredibly religious so it is difficult to know whether he believed in the concept of paradise and god. He had been raised a Catholic, but during his life his scientific mind had dragged him far away from religion and he did not seem to be a member of any church.

Many believe that he experimented with Kabbalah and that he nurtured a strong interest in it, yet rumours, often reported by Vasari, suggest that he was much more of a philosopher rather than a religious person. In the last years of his life, several sources report that he got closer to Catholicism.

When it came to religion, Leonardo was much too scientific and investigative; he would just go after things that would question, ever so subtly, the role of the church and perhaps its influence.

He was also a man who loved to explore different ideas and philosophies and that is exactly how he grew extremely close to Jewish mysticism and strongly approved of the Jewish concept of free will.

It is also equally interesting to note that the *Vitruvian Man* shares similarities with the Kabbalah tree of life.

In conversation with Silvano Vinceti, researcher and writer, founder and president of Comitato nazionale per la valorizzazione dei beni storici, culturali e ambientali

When it comes to the Mona Lisa, recent research by Silvano Vinceti, president of the Caravaggio Foundation, and his collaborator Stefania Romano has unveiled some interesting details. Following a number of studies, they announced a discovery concerning Leonardo and particularly the *Mona Lisa*.

According to Vinceti, from the National Committee for the Valorisation of Cultural Heritage (CONVAB), in 2011 the letter S was found in the *Mona Lisa*'s left eye, the letter L in her right eye, and, finally, the number 72 had also been located under the bridge in the backdrop of the painting itself, a fascinating discovery which opened the door to a number of mystical and religious interpretations, something Leonardo was also incredibly interested in.

This new discovery was added to several other hypotheses, hypotheses that want the *Mona Lisa* to be a man or a self-portrait of the author himself, while further theories label her as a pregnant woman or someone in mourning who can't manage a full smile yet.

The CONVAB carried out their research on high definition scanned images from Lumiere Technology in Paris. Vinceti, Romano and their team found the following elements in the *Mona Lisa* by excluding any reflexes and colours and isolating the letters to make them stand out more. According to an interview from 2011 released by Vinceti, the letter S could refer to a woman belonging to the Sforza family, while the letter L could refer to the artist, Leonardo, himself. During this interview, Vinceti stressed that the calligraphy is the same style used by Leonardo in his notebooks and that the number 72 is a very powerful number in Kabbalah (something Leonardo nurtured an interest in) Christianity and could be associated to the creation of the world and duality.

RS: What can you tell me about your discovery when it comes to the *Mona Lisa*?

SV: The discoveries made on Leonardo's famous painting are the letters S and L placed in the pupil of the right eye and in the pupil of the left eye, and the number 72 under one of the arches of the bridge located to the right of the woman depicted. In my book – *The Secret of the Mona Lisa* – you will find a detailed explanation of the meaning of the number 72, which refers to the letters S and L. The letters and 72 make up a clear esoteric, Kabbalistic message; the concept of androgyny is a reference to the two models that inspired Leonardo in the production of the famous painting (these models could be Salai and Lisa Gherardini).

RS: Leonardo was an intelligent man but also, and above all, mysterious; there are those who define him an alien, a member of the Order of the Templars, even someone from the future. Beyond the many conspiracies on the internet, who was in your opinion the real Leonardo da Vinci?

SV: That Leonardo lends himself to letting the imagination fly and create extremely risky mythologies is in part understandable. Every time a person is raised to a sacred or mythological level, he is changed, deformed by attributing to him characteristics that take inspiration from more religious and secular literature. Leonardo was certainly a person with great intelligence, an immense curiosity, a passion for creating and innovating. He was a person of great sensitivity who placed philosophy, science, technology and art at the centre of his life. Leonardo, the man, is a man with vices and virtues, successes and failures, amazing innovations and debts to the past, on an artistic, philosophical, religious, scientific and technical level. He was essentially a loner, he was different, or as he loved to label himself, 'a man without letters', injecting a subtle ironic, sarcastic and critical vein towards the scholars and academics of his time. By ethical choice and as a condition to satisfy his immense curiosity he wrote on various occasions that solitude, constant application, dedication and tenacity are essential characteristics for those who dedicate themselves to a lifetime of searching for truth and beauty, but the fundamental condition was *passion*. Historically, it does not appear that he was part of any esoteric, hermetic association or aggregation. Only if Leonardo is brought back from heaven to Earth can he be fully understood and appreciated. Otherwise, he is worshipped as a laic saint.

RS: Mysticism and Leonardo – what do you think?

SV: I don't think that Leonardo can be part of the mystical aesthetic experience – perhaps Michelangelo can, in particular in his last period of his life and artistic creation. He writes it himself in some poems of great importance to understand his process, particularly the sculptural one. Leonardo's notes on the art of painting are his direct explanation of what he really believes in, it's the experience that he considers the mother of all knowledge.

Among his various notes, the recommendation to painters is to use a mirror that faithfully reproduces things as they are, real, and it also suggests that painting is a mimesis of reality. He makes a clear distinction between natural and human reality and underlines how the strong interpretation of the human one must be based on physiognomy, on the ability to grasp the interiority of the pictorial subjects and translate it into corporeality. From this premise derives the importance given to the mimic, pantomime, to the importance of hands, eyes and smile play when it comes to painting. It is necessary to distinguish the symbolic language sign he uses to communicate his thought, his ideas, values and criticisms from the technical-pictorial aspect.

In addition to the *Mona Lisa*, the work that I consider of great communicative value of radical criticism of the papacy and clergy of his time is certainly his last pictorial effort: the *St John the Baptist*. In this work, he uses as a model his favourite pupil, Salai. It radically breaks a Christian-Catholic iconographic tradition that depicted the emaciated Baptist as a mystic, metaphysical and hermit. Leonardo's San Giovanni Battista is androgynous, sensual, ambiguous, dripping with carnal and material temptations. In this depiction shines Leonardo's criticism of the betrayal of Christ and divine commandments by the church of his time. If he had written it and disseminated it, it would have been subjected to the Inquisition Court.

RS: Can you tell me about the research on Lisa Gherardini and the research into her DNA?

SV: The primary purpose of the research on the mortal remains of Lisa Gherardini, known as Mona Lisa del Giocondo and wife of the influential silk worker Francesco del Giocondo, was to recover her bone remains, including the skull. The staff of the Committee was able, from the skull, to reconstruct the face with a marginal error which could range from five to ten per cent. If we had succeeded in the experiment, we could have made a comparison with the portrait of the famous painting and finally tried to give a technical solution to the unsolved riddle of the model used by Leonardo. For decades, many art historians around the world have given different and contradictory answers to this question. Personally, my thesis is that Leonardo made use of two models, the first Gherardini, the second Salai. Regarding this, I made several historical and scientific-technical arguments. Starting from Gherardini's death document (1542) which indicated her burial in the Franciscan complex of the Convent of Sant'Orsola, long research was carried out using an interdisciplinary staff coordinated by me. The staff had archaeological, biological, anthropological, historical, DNA, Carbon 14 and other expertise. The excavations lasted two years but we had to stop for a little while due to problems of financial resources.

Thanks to the convergence of the archaeological results with the reconstruction of the history of the Church of Sant'Orsula, used for the burial of noblewomen who had a close relative who became a third-order

Franciscan nun (see the recovery of many books updated by the different abbesses of the time with the deaths and the place of burials), we came to the conclusion that finding the mortal remains of Lisa Gherardini would have been highly probable.

This result is based on the convergence of historical data, the book of deaths, archaeological results and DNA. The incomplete remains of three women were found in a brick chest used for burials. The same DNA confirms, in its arc of probability, the period of death of Leonardo's model. Few were the burials of noblewomen in the small church inside the Franciscan complex. Gherardini had a nun daughter who took care of her in the last period of her life; she was a noblewoman and made many robust cash offers to the convent itself. Unfortunately, the absence of the skull did not allow us to perform the primary purpose of the research but we were allowed to recover partial mortal remains which brought us closer to the truth.

Chapter 14

Leonardo, the Icon

According to the Cambridge Dictionary's definition, an icon is a very famous person or a thing which can represent a set of beliefs or a way of life: Leonardo da Vinci was both. He was famous during his life; his reputation, both positive and negative, preceded him wherever he went. He was famous and he is famous after his time. He also became a more abstract concept which succeeded in detaching the human from his genius, his art, even his beautiful mind: he became an icon of art and the epitome of a genius.

Despite his unpredictable behaviour, he succeeded in building a legacy for being both an artist, leaving some of the most beautiful works of art, and as an inventor, an engineer for his Codices; a legacy so powerful as to become relevant to our days, defining a set of beliefs for the history of art, the scientific sector and everything else that stood out as being revolutionary, pioneering and much more advanced than his own time.

Often associated with anything that is mysterious, smart and often ineffable, Leonardo is the perfect modern icon and so are his works of art, which have been changed, reproduced and changed again to accommodate society, and sometimes its latest trends.

Even his name is iconic: Leonardo da Vinci, often used in our everyday language as an expression or meaning of incredible talent. It almost feels like Leonardo was born old, wise and talented. His icon was built, structured and successfully developed and disseminated through many and different media representations. It started with the first portrait ever painted of him; it is in this visuality, in the first image of Leonardo that we first see Leonardo the icon.

Birth of an icon

A face like Leonardo's is difficult to forget. It's the wise, old man we have seen plenty of times, the image we have learnt to associate with goodness, kindness, with the wise man who knows everything, fixes everything and whose main purpose in this life is helping others. He is the Dumbledore of the Renaissance, a reassuring, safe grandfather figure.

In all his portraits, Leonardo is never young; his beard is long, unruly, his eyes are deep, savvy and a reflection of the world he has seen and perhaps even of the one he has anticipated. This image cannot help but be stuck in our heads. He is not a lad, a young one who embraces life and its beauties. There is no trace of arrogance in this man, there is no trace of that fearless bravery, no trace of that young, light, athletic body. Leonardo's appearance, his most popular one, is the reflection of an old man that has become for us all the epitome of intelligence and wisdom, the epitome of Leonardo da Vinci.

The image we keep in our heads of Leonardo da Vinci is the final product of portraits usually taken by his apprentices (particularly those where he served as a model and 'commissioned' by Leonardo himself), his works of art and of a strong narrative established by Leonardo's early biographers.

It is interesting to note that the very first one who tries to give the world, even unconsciously, a different image of Leonardo is Verrocchio.

Verrocchio has the merit of showing the world a Leonardo who is younger, carefree, someone who had perhaps just started working at his studio, someone talented yet inexperienced and someone who could have easily been mistaken as one of his many apprentices.

Verrocchio's interpretation is not the one we would necessarily associate with Leonardo, the genius, the maestro in our heads. It's not the old man with long hair and deep eyes we have been accustomed to, there is no hat in this version, no long beard and no awareness in his stare, there is no depth. In Verrocchio's representation, Leonardo is just a boy, a model, he could be anyone.

The icon of Leonardo da Vinci is ineluctably attached to his official portraits. In all his portraits, often made by some of his scholars and students, Leonardo appears like a man who is older than his age and wiser than his time and perhaps that's exactly what he was.

In our collective imaginary, we are used to a Leonardo who had all the answers from science to the arts; he was the man who challenged, enriched and strived to always do better by looking at nature, what was around him, always by paying attention to the world, a lifetime student some would say. We never see him young, rebellious, with dreams and interests of his own, we see him as a mythological creature, a prophet perhaps, nothing short of a Nostradamus, someone who knew everything and, if he didn't, would just experiment hard enough to eventually understand it and explain it to others, disseminating his knowledge and his discoveries.

There was, after all, something almost imperceptible that Leonardo possessed, something no other painter or artist, not even his own teacher and friend Verrocchio or any other artist or genius of his time, ever had, something people were curious about, interested in or even slightly wary of. Leonardo was different to the rest of them, and his peculiarity didn't go unnoticed.

It is difficult to distinguish between the icon and the man. The real man, the real Leonardo, his thoughts, his ideas, his most genuine perspective on life has been greatly contaminated by what everyone thought of him and by media representations and other discoveries.

A recent discovery, particularly related to Leonardo's physical appearance, was recently made by the Royal Collection Trust; the discovery itself was a sketch made by one of Leonardo's students featuring his master. He was older then, probably much older than what we have ever seen; in this sketch, Leonardo is portrayed aged about 65 years old, with his long beard, one of his most recognisable facial traits. It is interesting to note, according to findings by the Royal Collection Trust, how peculiar it was for the time to keep such a long yet well-kept beard and how Leonardo, trendsetter that he was, had the power to re-introduce that particular look to fashion.

Leonardo's beard was also something that proved to be fundamental when identifying another portrait of him; the very first one drawn by another of Leonardo's pupils, painter Francesco Melzi.

It is equally important to note that both sketchers have portrayed a Leonardo lost in his own thoughts, in a world of nostalgia perhaps, as if he knew that the end was near and perhaps as if he knew that the rest of humanity was unprepared for what was to come. It's a detached Leonardo, yet maybe a Leonardo at his most real, accurate, perhaps a human version of himself.

Another element of extraordinary importance in creating Leonardo and his icon was the drafting of different biographies in his name, populated by different encounters which have given us a first foundational step in establishing Leonardo's reputation.

In Vasari's biography, in his write-up, and according to those people who met Leonardo and wrote about him, researched his world, his past and his life, there is a common vision, a perspective shared by many, which does nothing but confirm that everyone who met Leonardo had also been able to perceive something else in his persona, in his general being, a detail, a little wit in his eyes, in his expression and, eventually, the essence of someone who was perhaps much too advanced for the time and world, his and ours.

The myth of Leonardo, and of the person he was, started from the very beginning, not only with Vasari but also with his own students like Melzi, who by now we know kept his work alive and did his best to make sure it was protected in order to be safely delivered to our times.

Leonardo was a genius who needed to be protected, and so did his work. Everyone had an opinion about him and it's in this multiplicity of opinions that the icon of Leonardo starts to form.

Even Freud felt he had more to add when it came to Leonardo, with one of his most popular quotes about him being, 'Leonardo da Vinci was like a man who awoke too early in the darkness, while the others were all still asleep'. We can clearly understand what Freud means as Leonardo was not only a man who had made some significantly advanced discoveries and lent his genius to some of the most relevant, interesting works of art and science, but he was also a visionary, someone who is remembered for his futuristic approach to work, life and art, someone who was very much awake when everyone else was fast asleep. We can only begin to imagine the frustration of it all, being someone who could almost see the future, with his ideas, but could do very little about it.

Many have tried to capture Leonardo, the man. His stories and his work were also drafted by two highly admired, capable men of the time; the first was Italian biographer and physician Paolo Giovio, in his *Eulogies of Illustrious Men of Letters*, and the second, of course, was Giorgio Vasari, painter, architect, biographer and fellow genius of his time.

The first biographer, Giovio, has often been cited as being one of the first to ever talk about Leonardo and his world. Giovio, who was an avid art collector, is remembered for his works in Latin and for being an Italian historian. He settled in Rome in 1513 and, after gaining the favour of both Pope Leo X and of Cardinal Giulio de' Medici, he became Bishop of Nocera. He was one of the first to write a collection of biographies of famous men of his time, which included Leonardo.

It was, however, Vasari who first produced a biography that still today represents the very first step we have in tracing back Leonardo and his fascinating life. Unlike Giovio, who was an acquaintance of Leonardo's, Vasari never met him, yet he was able to depict the very first portrait of him and his life. Vasari, a fellow polymath, was probably one of the most suitable candidates to record Leonardo and his world. He was the first to understand his genius, only by living in his world, breathing his art in Florence and witnessing his reputation unfold. He was not scared to research and travel in order to produce his biographies of some of the most important men of his and our time, something that even included the likes of Michelangelo and Cimabue. It is because of Vasari that we have one of the first chances to read about the genius that was Leonardo da Vinci. Vasari made a strong contribution towards creating the icon of Leonardo da Vinci and of those other painters he wrote about in his biographies.

Yet Leonardo da Vinci was mostly made an icon by his own work. It's his work that sanctified him to iconography levels. We consider him a genius because of his inventions, and call him mysterious because of how different his works of art are, not only because of their symbolism but also because they are shrouded in a cloud of mystery no one has ever quite fully grasped.

Leonardo and the *Mona Lisa*

She looks at you, but does she really? You will never know. Long brown hair, a woman, or maybe not. She looks at you but, again, does she really? Is she really paying attention or is she miles away, looking at something way beyond our understanding? Some say she is a man, others that she is a prostitute, a friend of the man who had the audacity to freeze her smile in time, for everyone to see, admire and, yes, even question. According to many she is nothing more than a commission from a man in love, she is the lover of an important man, someone whose passion had led him to that particular artist, or perhaps she is the author himself, in a mirror-image of his genius, she is a mystery, a gaze, a deep gaze, chasing, hunting you for centuries.

There is something beautiful, fascinating, yet slightly scary about her smile, which many believe to be a product of a medical condition, perhaps teeth issues or something related to her thyroid. There is also something charming about the way she seems to attract her audience. The overused word enigmatic comes to mind, yet there is really no better adjective to even begin to make sense of Leonardo da Vinci's most famous work of art, the *Mona Lisa*.

Mona Lisa was and still is for many just another Florentine merchant's wife, Lisa del Giocondo, but for others she truly is a testament to Leonardo's genius, talent and understanding of the female universe, perhaps; something that was incredibly dear to him, something that he had already explored in several of his works, portraits that stood out for being different, which had the merit of transferring to the canvas some of the most interesting and beautiful Renaissance women of the time.

If Leonardo is an icon, the *Mona Lisa* is an icon on its own, a product of Leonardo's imagination that has become equally famous and a real trendsetter, capable of perfectly interpreting different eras and societies.

The painting is a portrait of a woman. There are many points of view on that woman. Her identity is a mystery but sometimes so is her gender. She has big and soft hands and she wears a veil over her head, which some believe to be a symbol of maternity. The thing that shocks people the most, perhaps making everyone feel a little uneasy about what otherwise would be just another portrait of a Renaissance woman, is the stare, *Mona Lisa*'s stare. It's a little trick by Leonardo, proof of that humorous personality he had. *Mona Lisa*'s eyes follow and chase you from the moment you step into the room. Yet, when you look closely, she is not looking at you directly, she is not looking at us in the eyes, yet her eyes do seem to follow us, no matter where we are in the room. It's disorienting, it feels weird, yet we cannot stop looking at her.

Mona Lisa is so mysterious that no one ever agrees when it comes to where she is from and who she is. Another hypothesis concerning her origin is that the model for the painting was a deceased woman, someone Leonardo could have only painted by memory as he had met her once. According to this theory, Leonardo painted her as a commission from Giuliano de' Medici, and the woman in question is Pacifica Brandano.

Pacifica was the woman Giuliano loved more than anyone, his mistress. She died in childbirth and Giuliano had the painting made for their child together, Ippolito, so that he could know what his mother looked like.

An interesting 2011 article from the *Guardian* explores Leonardo and the extraordinary female universe he created, arguing that in direct comparison to his predecessors or even his contemporaries including Verrocchio, Leonardo had a tendency of conferring on women a tridimensionality which had never been explored quite like that by anyone else.

In his four different portraits of women, *Mona Lisa* included, Leonardo finally managed to paint women as they were, with their own personality, something which was rather feminist for the time as it was not in line with the patriarchal society of the Renaissance. *Mona Lisa* was openly flirtatious and so was her smile, something which was in line with the portraits taken of the women of the time, but she also stood out for her enigmatic smile; a woman no man can control, not even her creator.

Mona Lisa had a personality; she was not just a Renaissance woman posing for another portrait commissioned by another man who wanted to court her, possibly own her. *Mona Lisa* was a woman with a story and possibly, as most people believe, a secret – something she hadn't perhaps disclosed to the men in her life. Many researchers believe that she was pregnant.

Leonardo, with his works, his sensitivity, succeeded in finally depicting women for what they were: articulate creatures, perhaps more complex than men could ever possibly begin to imagine.

The best thing about the *Mona Lisa* is that her fame has almost become bigger than Leonardo's; she is an icon in her own right and her appearance has been manipulated several times to accommodate concepts or, in the social media era, different memes online.

It is interesting to look at different versions of her that want her to turn into other women, perhaps just as famous – for example the *Mona Lisa* seen through the lens of Frida Kahlo, another icon, another powerful woman whose image, as well, has been altered endlessly. In one of these particular Frida Kahlo-*Mona Lisa* representations, Mona Lisa does not lose her basis facial traits, and that is proof of being a strong icon, you can always recognise her, no matter what kind of elements are constantly added to her appearance. In this Frida Kahlo version, the *Mona Lisa* still keeps her pose, the smile and the attitude. The smile is the most important thing and that is what makes her recognisable in the first place. Like the original, you cannot shake that glance off, it follows you around and chases you no matter where you go, her eyes are on you. Much like the original, that stare, a little disheartening or embarrassing, intrusive at the very least, is everywhere.

But one thing is certain: this lady is not the *Mona Lisa*. Elaborate earrings, ruffled curly hair, a hairband, a monkey as her trustworthy companion of adventures, thick eyebrows and upper lip hair: she is a crossover between *Mona Lisa* and Frida. Even the background is not the same – forget the placid river, this has dissolved into something more tropical, something which reminds us of Frida and of the style of some of her most famous paintings.

The *Mona Lisa* is so strong that it is possible to use her, to use her appearance, her world, Leonardo's world, and push a different message out, and by doing so, establish a different narrative. Frida Kahlo is not the only one to help herself to the *Mona Lisa*, of course. There are so many media interpretations and versions of her online. By searching in Google Images for 'altered *Mona Lisa*', anyone will find an extraordinary number of versions of the famous painting by Leonardo, some funny, others inspired by movies, music, art or anything that is topical or on-trend.

There's the *Mona Lisa* who distinguishes herself with a rather rock and roll style and perhaps approach to life who holds onto her guitar; there's a sad *Mona Lisa* without her famous smile, a naked *Mona Lisa* and even a Simpsons and a LEGO *Mona Lisa*. She really is everywhere, a timeless icon of both modernity and style.

It is interesting to note how even big brands have managed to use *Mona Lisa* and alter her to fit their marketing campaigns, something which was particularly interesting to see in a recent marketing campaign by LEGO which used different works of art including *Mona Lisa*. The campaign by advertising agency Geometry Global won the Cannes Gold Lion in 2014 and put together LEGO recreations of famous masterpieces which included the *Mona Lisa*, *The Lady with an Ermine* and many other works of art including the *Girl with a Pearl Earring*.

It just goes to confirm that Leonardo's art has reached a timeless status, something that would go and eventually inspire marketing campaigns. The *Mona Lisa* is probably one of the most popular works of art by Leonardo da Vinci as well as the one which has been changed, altered and disseminated by the media and now social media the most. When it's not in pop art colours in an Andy Warhol version, it's often adorned with a touch of extra colour, extra personalities or even extra people; no one ever leaves her alone and the ironic thing is that the more altered and amended she gets, the more famous she becomes; the more versions of her seem to come up out of nothing, the more famous her creator Leonardo becomes, a true testament of his genius and a pure and simple icon of our time.

He is unequivocally connected to the *Mona Lisa*, he established a narrative, a mystery that has been going on for more than 500 years, he is the man behind the portrait, the father behind the birth of her icon and the man behind its iconography, orchestrating its success by adding a smile that has fascinated people for generations.

The continuous reinterpretations of the *Mona Lisa* don't take away from her iconography or her value but keep on adding to her public persona – she is like a celebrity who continually re-invents herself.

We cannot help but remember that she is not just another painting, she is Leonardo's *Mona Lisa*; no one else could have ever conceived of such a strange yet addictive creature and so her icon, her power, is rubbed off on Leonardo and vice versa in a constant cultural interchange. They make each other always more relevant, on-trend and deserving of mythological status. She is the woman Leonardo almost made alive on his canvas, the only woman of his life, it's Leonardo himself, it's a prostitute, a lover, it's everyone and no one, but by wondering about her past, her behaviour, society cannot help but fall always more in love with her magnetism; a magnetism so palpable as to inspire new, modern artists, as well, who keep changing her, giving their own interpretations.

The *Mona Lisa* is so iconic that even the street artist Banksy couldn't resist suggesting his very own personal version. He did it twice, each time giving his very personal interpretation of da Vinci's work of art. The first time was in 2004, when he had the audacity to put his version of Leonardo's work up in the Louvre itself: his version was exactly like Leonardo's *Mona Lisa*, with the only difference being in the smile – Banksy's *Mona Lisa* had a yellow smiley face. This work was called *Mona Lisa Smile* and sold in 2006 for more than £56,000.

Another reinterpretation of *Mona Lisa* by Banksy was *Mona Lisa Bazooka*, which first appeared in West London in 2007. In this version, *Mona Lisa* wears a headset and she is aiming a rocket launcher. It is not the first time that *Mona Lisa* has been given an even stronger personality than what Leonardo originally planned for her.

The most interesting moment for Mona Lisa and her constant reinterpretations occurred during the COVID-19 crisis in 2020, something not even Leonardo could have prepared her for. At this time, there were several representations of the *Mona Lisa*, often created by non-professional people with different apps and distributed on several social media including and particularly Instagram, which, with Twitter, from its visual perspective, succeeded in creating a range of different, new narrative scenarios – narratives which cared very little about time or space.

In one particular meme, available from the Instagram account 'Art is my fashion', Leonardo da Vinci's *Mona Lisa* can be seen in a different setting than the one we usually see her in. In this one, she looks dishevelled, she has been left in the museum on her own now that the visitors are gone, with no clothes, smoking a cigarette, and holding on to a guitar. She is also wearing sunglasses hiding her famous stare, she looks like a rock star, but most importantly she appears to be feeling like a rock star. There is also a glass of wine in the background.

It's a different perspective on the *Mona Lisa*, but maybe not so much – it's a reinterpretation of the anarchic nature many people seem to see in her. She has always been seen as a rebel but this time, with tattoos on her body, it is like she has fully, finally become herself, or a 2020 version of herself. Tired of posing for museum visitors, she is just embracing who she is; maybe she is free for the first time, free from their glances, she who is often accused of stalking her visitors with her mysterious stare is now free from the museum cage she has been imprisoned in. COVID-19 has finally given her the peace she so strongly yearned for.

The only thing unaltered about this situation is Leonardo's beautiful landscape in the background – it's there, unchanged, which serves to remind us of the one who started everything and gave life to this enigmatic woman, brought us the indomitable creature that is *Mona Lisa*: Leonardo, the maestro.

Another picture available from 'Art is my fashion' shows an even more rebellious side of the *Mona Lisa*, an even more adventurous version of Leonardo's creature.

In this particular reinterpretation, she is pictured in a car with painter Vincent Van Gogh, smoking, as is Van Gogh. Her blouse is open and she shows her bra to those in the audience. She just stares at us, relaxed, not a care in the world; who knows where she is going, and what would Leonardo say if he saw her like that? His mysterious Renaissance woman driving away in a car with another painter.

There are several steps for a personality to become an icon, and often death plays a vital part, as it not only immortalises the personality, but it also sanctifies their work, bringing him or her to icon levels. In the case of the *Mona Lisa*, not being a real person but a portrait of someone who lived over 500 years ago, her icon status is purely attributed to her, it's in the legend, the myth and the mystery Leonardo created around her: her background, her family and the largely unknown circumstances of her 'birth'. It is this essential element of not knowing that creates or has the ability and the merit of producing multiple different narratives, with the mystery of the *Mona Lisa* becoming the mystery of Leonardo.

Despite knowing about his life, his work, his discoveries, there is still a strong allure of mystery about him, about his intelligence, his pioneering works, the lack of proof about him; Leonardo, as a person, his constant stream of consciousness, divulged through his notebooks. We are left with an eagerness when it comes to his life, we want to know more about him, the different representations in art, pop culture, books, TV series, his death centuries ago.

There are many things we could say about Leonardo da Vinci but 'icon' is probably one of the most common; his works, discoveries and personalities have been sealed in our collective imaginary, becoming an icon, used, reused and often overused by the media and its channels including social media, which have the merit of making him even more down to Earth, bringing his genius to our use, using his work to question society, to explain how we feel or just to illustrate a meme on Twitter.

Whether useful or culturally relevant, it does not matter – Leonardo, the *Mona Lisa* and his other works are icons in the making, which keep changing and transforming themselves.

Even Leonardo da Vinci's appearance became iconic: his long red hair, his beautiful face, his height, something that not everyone could grasp which made Leonardo the icon we have learnt to love but never fully understood, and that adds to his iconic value as well.

It is not just his life, of course, even his works are shrouded in mystery – the *Mona Lisa*, *The Last Supper* – and it doesn't help that, 500 years after his death, we keep finding missing pieces of the puzzles that were his works of art, including paintings underneath his most famous paintings.

The representation of his persona has been full of contradictions and celebrated thanks to different forms of media including movies, books and TV series in his name. He boasts of such popularity, 500 years later, that not a day goes by without someone mentioning his name, opening a Twitter account with his works, or doing something using his pictures. There are several social media accounts under his name available on the internet; disseminating his ideas, talking mostly about his works of art, but also about the different sketches that have been found, often based on paintings he would later produce, or ideas he never quite finished.

And this is the beauty of Leonardo's works; they are so relevant and personal to each and every one of us that everyone, artists in particular, feels they can leave or add something of them to his paintings. Leonardo's legacy does not stop at his canvas but goes way beyond that.

In 2020, for example, following the COVID-19 crisis and with most museums closed, the Louvre launched an immersive experience entitled '*Mona Lisa*: Beyond the Glass', which offered an up-close look at the painting by utilising VR technology; it was a precious insight which had the benefit of showing *Mona Lisa* in 3D. Finally, she moved – the only thing Leonardo could not give her was granted to her by the professionals at the Louvre; this was just further confirmation of how Leonardo's works change and evolve, being so flexible as to manage to adapt themselves to meet the needs of every society and time, even those of 2020, during an international crisis.

Another meme which also became famous during the COVID-19 crisis is the one which sees the *Mona Lisa* in four different poses which aim to describe the four different stages of quarantine, which were the most common stages people went through during the lockdown. The first image shows the *Mona Lisa* in her iconic, classic pose, not a hair out of place, signalling the first stage of quarantine where everything was still OK and people were still taking selfies and apparently taking care of their wellbeing. The second image shows *Mona Lisa* as she flips her hair to one side and takes a more sensual pose as she tries to take a selfie. The third image features a *Mona Lisa* completely dishevelled, tired of quarantine and perhaps looking forward to going back to some level of normality. The fourth features an overweight *Mona Lisa* signalling the final stage of quarantine, in which most people felt tired and frustrated.

The message is clear; even *Mona Lisa* was going through a lockdown and, most importantly, through its most popular stages, from trying to keep it together to total boredom and frustration.

The reason is very simple: Leonardo's *Mona Lisa* has become one of the girls, she is the icon and the myth and, according to social media users in 2020, she needs to be involved in the crisis, stuck at home like everyone else, taking a selfie like just like everyone else and succumbing to boredom like everyone else on social media. *Mona Lisa* is modern, she was modern back in the Renaissance, and she still is modern, frozen in her youth, her smile contemplating, teasing, knowing about everyone and everything. She also makes an appearance on social media with someone called @WenzlerPowers saying that Dolly Parton writing 'I Will Always Love You' and 'Jolene' on the same day is so mind-blowing that it can only be compared to da Vinci finishing the *Mona Lisa* and writing 'Jolene' on the same day. The *Mona Lisa* is an institution, an icon, to which everything that is a masterpiece, important, full of grandeur, one of a kind, is compared to; interesting also to compare Dolly Parton, a feminist icon, to da Vinci's work of art. This makes the *Mona Lisa* a modern icon who is constantly nourished, century after century, by those taking the time to collocate her within a social trend of the moment.

There is, in fact, adaptability in the *Mona Lisa*; she can be anyone and for anyone, a blank canvas onto which people project their own being, their own insecurities and personalities.

Leonardo's works have become iconic, icons of irreverence, capable of creating the right opportunity for reflection. The *Mona Lisa* makes us feel dissociated from reality, she puts us in a situation which leaves us feeling restless, while questions start to populate our minds, consciously and perhaps unconsciously: why is she looking at us, why is she staring, why does she follow our every move with such insistence, why did Leonardo paint a painting with such important, defining details? Unfortunately, these questions will always be a mystery, but what is not a mystery is the fact that, once created, this same painting became an icon of style, no matter which society judges, questions or even alters it. No matter if she is going through lockdown, if she has been altered by Banksy, Warhol or any other artist, it matters very little if she is a Twitter star or takes selfies on Instagram – *Mona Lisa* is a strong icon on her own.

The *Mona Lisa* is, of course, not the only work of Leonardo which is continuously changed and altered to fit a purpose, to make us reflect or question society. Another one, perhaps even more complex in narrative and style, is *The Last Supper*.

Leonardo and *The Last Supper*

Another painting which has had the merit of putting Leonardo on the iconography map, making him an icon and becoming an icon on its own, is *The Last Supper*.

The Last Supper often goes through changes and accommodates marketing or social media needs to explain concepts, to make them bolder and perhaps to question what we think we know. The painting's concept is challenging already; it follows the moment Jesus Christ says his famous words 'I tell you, one of you will betray me', and freezes the reaction of the apostles as they talk among themselves and come up with different ideas, pointing fingers at each other on the canvas. It's a hush-hush conversation, a narrative which is incredibly powerful and has the power of showing men and their weaknesses. Yet, despite the biblical message, it has been easily manipulated and altered to fit different purposes and messages online. There are images and memes of the 'Christmas Last Supper' with all the apostles wearing colourful party hats, and a more outrageous one with the pole-dance pole right in the middle of the table.

Being a far more religious painting, *The Last Supper* has also been subjected to different polemics, especially when, recently, a famous artist published a version of the painting with a Turkish chef taking the place of Jesus. The painting and its characters are still relevant and often used to spark conversations and deal with different topics.

It is a painting featuring two important events, the one happening on the actual canvas and the one unfolding in one of these different reinterpretations.

Even more dramatic events are shown in one of the most recent interpretations of Leonardo's *Last Supper*. It is the case of artist Jose Manuel Ballester, who launched a series of paintings in which he removed their main characters, leaving still and empty rooms instead. Emptying *The Last Supper* as well, he showed Leonardo's masterpiece with no apostles, creating a powerful effect. Especially when it comes to paintings which have been consecrated to our collective imaginary as being rich and populated by different characters and their worlds, Ballester's experiment leaves us feeling uneasy and almost fearful; particularly considering how strong Leonardo's painting narratives are, and with *The Last Supper* being a painting about whispered conversations and strong characters. The general feeling is of strong dissociation.

During the COVID-19 crisis, memes were also fundamental, and Leonardo's paintings were some of the most altered and used; an interesting one about *The Last Supper* shows the party happening on a Zoom video chat, with Jesus checking if Judas is still online; a situation many people found themselves in when they were forced to go in full remote working mode during the crisis. The connotation is simple: the apostles are us, they are human beings and, much like us, they have been used to express the frustration of everyday life, including the COVID crisis.

Another interesting meme which is the product of the COVID crisis is the idea of the participants in *The Last Supper* being fined, with policemen interrupting the apostles from carrying on with their last meal, and charging them with gathering in a large group.

Before COVID, *The Last Supper* has been used to express different moments in life or trends within the society of the time: that is how we have different reinterpretations of the same painting, from baseball players interrupting the moment, to members of the cast of *The Office* taking the place of the apostles, or American politicians, with Donald Trump posing as Jesus.

The Last Supper has also been used as a pretext for parodies in different art spoofs which have the same characters, the apostles and Jesus, playing different roles and even change their personalities to accommodate a new message: these involve Jesus jumping on the table and playing the guitar, the *Looney Tunes* replacing the apostles or characters from *The Simpsons* to Disney films.

Much like the *Mona Lisa*, no matter how many times *The Last Supper* goes through different manipulations and interpretations, and whether those endless versions are shared online or in video or even broadcast, the main message goes back to Leonardo's original work and reinforces his value as a timeless icon.

The Last Supper was not the only example of how Leonardo's icon was disseminated through his own works of art. Leonardo, his life, his universe and his work have also become part of the mainstream media, thanks to different representations in TV series and films.

Leonardo, TV and movies

Leonardo and his world have been interpreted and re-interpreted several times. Images of Leonardo did not only become popular during the 2020 COVID-19 crisis but had started to make an appearance even before then with documentaries, TV series and movies; even when it came to children's television, Leonardo and the Renaissance more generally made an appearance in the shape of the *Teenage Mutant Ninja Turtles*, whose main characters were named after the Renaissance's four principal artists: Leonardo, Michelangelo, Donatello and Raffaello.

It's not just television and children's programmes; many other media, from TV series to movies and documentaries, have used Leonardo and his works of art as a way to express trends.

The figure of Leonardo, his world, his discoveries and his life have also been at the centre of different media representations; one in particular has been *Da Vinci's Demons*, which had the merit of showing a different side of Leonardo.

In this TV series, Leonardo is a man of passions – intelligent, sarcastic, charming, and a ladies' man. The TV series perfectly extrapolates the essence of Leonardo, an engineer, someone who was not interested in painting much but who was more interested in his inventions, in finding funds, in finding a patron who believed in him and his works and especially how these inventions, despite being extravagant, sometimes dangerous and expensive, could be of benefit to other people. In the TV series, Leonardo is portrayed as a genius in everything he did, but mostly as someone who was a man of science and who was also provided with a strong instinct.

He is also a young man, which comes in direct opposition with the image we have of Leonardo. To see him portrayed by Tom Riley in a young, dashing way is not what we necessarily expect to see when it comes to Leonardo da Vinci; yet it is equally important to see a different point of view on his life and remember that, before being a genius, he was a man and, in this case, a young man who was full of life and promise.

TV series and documentaries are not the only representations celebrating Leonardo and his world; films are also a popular choice when it comes to exploring Leonardo and his life.

Io Leonardo is a more recent homage to Leonardo da Vinci and his universe, his works and his whole persona. It's an art movie and it stands as a movie that is a perfect representation of Leonardo, particularly looking at how his mind worked.

The film has the ability to distinguish itself from other media versions and interpretations of Leonardo's works for different reasons. It's an arty interpretation of the genius, of his personality and of how he did what he did, how he conceived his work and how his brilliant mind worked.

The film has the ability and the merit to capture Leonardo's volatile personality and unstable behaviour, talking about his life but mostly focusing on what was in his mind, how his brain worked, taking the viewer on a fascinating journey which psychoanalyses Leonardo a little and makes everyone understand a bit more about his persona. It's chronological, yet theme-based, by also making sure to include different, sometimes challenging episodes of his life.

Io Leonardo focuses on different themes including Leonardo's curiosity and his interest in everything, particularly in what he didn't know but felt he could go ahead and explore on his own; by studying, researching and just continuing his journey by always being a student first.

Portrayed by Italian actor Luca Argentero, once again, we witness a Leonardo who is a young version of himself, he is not the wise man we have been accustomed to. It seems that new media versions and reinterpretations of Leonardo and his life have been trying hard to shift the archaic idea that wants him to be just a wise old man. At some point in his life, he was young, he was human and it was at that time in his life that he was capable of creating some extraordinary inventions and works of art.

The most interesting thing about *Io Leonardo* is the perspective from which it is told, the presence of the conscience of Leonardo, someone physically constantly vocalising Leonardo's inner thoughts, which is the most interesting thing about Leonardo: why he does what he does, why he decides to explore one particular area of knowledge over another one, how Leonardo becomes Leonardo da Vinci, how constantly questioning himself, reasoning about the world and its meaning turned him from simple painter or artist to genius and icon.

Leonardo would always question society, the world, trying to understand what he couldn't at first. In the movie, he establishes an inner dialogue, which is strong and is a perfect interpretation of his notes found in his notebooks, treasuring his best inventions but most importantly his most secret thoughts.

Io Leonardo explores different elements in the world of Leonardo and looks at his life from a different perspective, perhaps never used before. In the movie, Leonardo is what we would expect him to be: a genius, so creative, so quick in the way he reasons and produces that he cannot stand still – literally, as Argentero moves, walks, and gives life to the Italian genius, and figuratively, as his mind travels through his ideas, his inventions and his own being. His mind tells his story using actor Francesco Pannofino as the voice of his consciousness. It's a deep voice that comes from what we would expect Leonardo's soul to perhaps sound like in real life. It's a visual journey which takes us from Vinci to his last home in France, giving us the opportunity to learn about his best and most famous works of art, as he travels and changes patrons, from Lorenzo de' Medici to Sforza and Cesare Borgia. In *Io Leonardo*, several topics are explored including Leonardo's love and appreciation for nature, and how much time he spent looking at the different ways nature could serve his painting and how he could use nature for his inventions.

It is in the *Last Supper* scene that *Io Leonardo* reaches its peak; it's a scene that perfectly embodies Leonardo and his genius, based on Leonardo's words and notes. It cannot help but be an intimate moment, something only a genius would conceive. It's a moment of pure narrative, and of particular interest is the way he talks to those who would then be portrayed in his painting as the apostles. We can see how Leonardo's mind worked, how it established relations, how it would connect the dots in his head, how he would, as explored in the movie, follow people around in the city, looking for those faces, the faces for his painting, and in the *Last Supper*'s case, the faces he would then use for his apostles.

By telling these people what to do, how to behave, the da Vinci in *Io Leonardo* is giving us once again a glimpse of his mind and his thoughts. One particular quote from the movie says, 'I tuoi apostoli sono vivi, sono umani, siamo noi,' which means, 'Your apostles are alive, are human, they are us,' which perfectly embodies Leonardo and his interest and efforts to understand human nature.

It is interesting to note that Leonardo chose a particular moment when painting *The Last Supper* which is the moment Jesus informs his incredulous apostles that one particular person at that very same table will betray him. In *Io Leonardo*, it is the preparation in Leonardo's head that is represented, how the narrative takes place in his consciousness first and how he can finally see the scene taking place right before his eyes. It is the culmination of his studies: when he was following people in the street, when he was studying human nature, when he was looking in the crowd searching for those faces, for those one day he would place as characters in his paintings, he was trying to humanise them so that we could perhaps find ourselves in his works.

Another aspect analysed by *Io Leonardo* is the almost total absence of emotions from his side; as he lists his mother's funeral expenses in his notes, Leonardo doesn't give away any emotion, it is as though he is listing something which is not of any particular importance to him.

We know by now that Leonardo's relationship with his mother was strained, he wasn't close to her, yet it is the almost total absence of his emotions from his notebooks that puzzles the rest of us, leaving us unsure about him and his feelings. We know by now that he was a funny, humorous man who would find joy and humour in everything he saw, in everything his stare would rest on, but there is hardly ever any note which would confirm a passion, a love towards something or someone, a mother, a friend, a lover, anyone, and in listing the expenses for his mother's funeral, there is once again confirmation of not only his detachment towards his maternal figure but also a continuous avoidance when it came to sharing his true feelings, or at least writing them down in his notes. In the movie, the voice of Leonardo's conscience thunders, 'Ti spaventa essere umano?' ('Are you afraid of being human?'), and again, 'Affronti così le tue emozioni?' ('Is this how you deal with your feelings?'). In the movie, the list is also defined as cold, almost impersonal, and that is exactly what it is, just a note, just something Leonardo makes a note of, a cold list of the exact amount of money he spent for his mother's funeral.

Nature is a strong element in the movie; it's an art movie that has the merit of projecting Leonardo's insides on the outside, making us see, perhaps for the very first time, who Leonardo was and how infinite his ideas were, how thirsty he always seemed to be when it came to knowledge and how interested he was in everything that surrounded him, from human beings to nature. The movie is the most interesting representation we have of Leonardo and his conscience, perhaps the only one, something that finally shows us the maestro as someone who would just keep going and never stop when it came to learning, exploring and bringing something new and different to the table every single day, even if this brought him problems and fame for being lazy and unreliable.

He was quite the opposite – he was precise, he was scrupulous, probably too scrupulous in his work and that is why things took time or never quite came to an end, remaining unfinished.

Leonardo himself, his life, feels unfinished; it is a narrative that keeps evolving, changing, adapting to who we are, us, the faces in the crowd he chased, unchanged, frozen in his paintings, and that is probably why, when we look at his work, we find something that tells us about us.

It is in the constant reinterpretation of him and his works of art that Leonardo can be found; it is almost like he is the pure expression of constant reinvention, both his own and that of his works, everything he has done is pure clay in the hands of the society of the time, and of our time, that does what it pleases, and we do as we please with him, with his inventions, with his works, by changing and playing with his icon. In *Io Leonardo*, Leonardo is always, once again, modern in the eyes of the spectator; he is the spectator.

In conversation with Jesus Garces Lambert, director of *Io Leonardo* (Sky d'Arte Italia, Progetto Immagine, Lucky Red)

RS: What really attracted you to the figure of Leonardo da Vinci in the first place, and how did the idea for a movie come about?

JGL: When you start doing a movie about a character like Leonardo da Vinci, the main thing is that you need to deal with this idea which is basically that everybody thinks they know him and you also think you know him. To make a film about Leonardo, telling just what he did, was not what we had envisioned for this movie, we wanted to try to get to who this character is, what's in his mind, what made him so special, what made him so curious.

The way we usually work with Sky Arte (Cinema d'Arte Sky) is that the investigation has to go as if it was an academic study; we choose a side we want to understand about this character and we do a very intensive investigation. Only after processing all this information do we start creating a narrative line. As a director, I believe that, if you go see a movie, it has to be an experience. If you pay the entrance fee to see a film, you need to feel that you leave the theatre gaining something, that it changed you in a way, emotionally, intellectually, spiritually. Before starting to work on the mind of Leonardo, we started having different conversations with Pietro Marani, one of the greatest experts on Leonardo internationally. He gave us a frame to understand Leonardo and to establish who Leonardo truly was. The first thing he told us was, 'You have to read Leonardo, not read about Leonardo' – reading what he wrote, what he designed, the way he organised his work. So the first thing the screenwriter – Sara Mossetti – did was to start reading the Codices, Leonardo's Codices, creating a map into Leonardo's mind. Then together with Cosetta Lagani (former artistic director from Cinema Sky Arte), a line was drawn: it was decided to narrate Leonardo's mind, to try to understand how it works, not what Leonardo did but how that amazing mind worked. We spoke with neuro-specialists, trying to understand how the human brain functions, and with all this information we drew a narrative line that couldn't be chronological but rather more an association of ideas where the spectator could start thinking as Leonardo did.

RS: In terms of the opening scene, we are seeing the cave for the first time, and that's quite an important moment in Leonardo's life and explains how Leonardo used to approach different experiences. It's an interesting concept of fear and desire. Why did you make the choice of opening the scene and starting from the cave?

JGL: The film has a circular structure. In the beginning, the film establishes the cave as a metaphor for his biggest fear, which is not to be able to get the knowledge he desires, and at the end of the movie, which shows the end of his life, he realises that he never controlled nature, because he never fully understood it, as it is impossible for a man to do. The opening scene sets the milestone from where his existence moves. For all his life, Leonardo tried to understand what was around him. Being an illegitimate son, he didn't have access to education and didn't have the tools to study the books written in Latin, so trying to understand what surrounded him made nature his only teacher. Starting from the cave was an important moment as it also breaks all the standard 'prototypes' you have about Leonardo as an old and 'saggio' wise man, a dusty old man who thinks he knows everything about the world. Leonardo was a man who had fears, who had passions and who had objectives that were never fulfilled, and this is the Leonardo you can see in the film. What was Leonardo's biggest fear? He was scared to not understand the world, nature, not to control nature.

RS: It is interesting that in the movie you start with nature and you finish with nature as well at the end of the movie when nature overcomes Leonardo. That room scene is incredibly powerful, how did you manage to obtain that effect? What made you decide to go for a move that is so artistically and visually powerful? What made you decide to go for an arty movie for this particular theme?

JGL: The main idea is that you cannot make a movie that speaks about art without the movie itself becoming an art piece. We are talking about a theatrical movie, not a television movie, you need to make a piece that can stand on its own and tell another story that is not necessarily the story that you already know. As a director, when you are telling a story about art, you have translated the emotion you feel when you are in a museum standing in front of a painting. You have to create an artistic experience with the film universe and transport the viewer into another dimension

152

On the film, we are inside Leonardo's mind, and what better space could it be than his chamber of mirrors, an octagonal space made of mirrors that reflects all faces of whoever stands in the middle, and that in a symbolic language represents all of Leonardo's faces. It was a space where everything changed, and moved, it had its own life, it was always the same space but always different.

Leonardo was a remarkable engineer and I tried to take his knowledge into the scene. In terms of special effects, all you see in the room was created on the actual set, in an analogical way avoiding the digital universe.

RS: Do you think that is how Leonardo's mind worked, that he had this constant dialogue with himself, challenging himself, questioning what he did on a regular basis?

JGL: You can never separate your mind from your feelings and emotions. The way Leonardo thought was a result of his emotional needs. He had not been recognised by his father, not even after his death, he was taken away from his mother when he was a child, so he had some strong emotional needs that he had to cover, and the way he did it was by focusing on satisfying his thirst for knowledge, learning from what surrounded him. In the latest years, we have more tools to study our past, tools such as psychology, psychoanalysis and much more, so I am convinced that you can't speak about his mind without speaking about his emotional needs.

I was surprised that the more I read about Leonardo the more human I found him and the more similar to us. In the film Leonardo is set up as a 39-year-old very beautiful man, elegant, intelligent, funny and vain, as a manuscript of the time describes him. During the film he never gets old or changes because he is always inside his mind, everything around him grows, all the characters in his life evolve but he remains as you see him on that very first scene.

RS: And speaking about his emotions, something that really shocked him and changed him was the Saltarelli affair and you manage to show that moment incredibly well, you feel his pain and you kind of feel what he went through, do you think that episode really had some kind of impact and influence on his life?

JGL: I am certain that it had a strong impact on him – at the time sodomy was punishable by the death penalty so imagine being the son of a notary

153

and be publicly accused of that, it was a big shame for the family. He started denying all the emotions, all his sexual desires studying the nature of desire as if it was a machine, he studies the way sexuality works in a scientific way, saying only, 'Beasts can let themselves abandon to desire.' It is amazing that if you read all the pages he wrote – more than 6,000 – he never mentioned anything about his personal life.

RS: One of the most interesting scenes in the movie is the one with *The Last Supper*, how did you come up with that idea?

JGL: The idea for the scene of *The Last Supper* came from Leonardo himself. He left lots of traces in different pages of the studies for this painting, he wrote every little detail he planned for the picture, what the apostles were thinking, how they were reacting. It was all written by him, as was all the dialogue in the film – the words spoken by Leonardo as played by Luca Argentero are from Leonardo himself. The idea of the scene was to follow exactly Leonardo's indications and to be as close as possible to how he worked. It seemed, in the beginning, an easy task, but as always when you approach Leonardo nothing is what it seems to be. For example, Leonardo was a master of optical illusion so to replicate the same frame as *The Last Supper* I had to study exactly the position of the camera, the lens that I had to use, the position of the apostles and all the details on the scene, but what surprised me the most was the position of the table; to get the same optical effect Leonardo gave to *The Last Supper* we had to give an angle to the table of around 45 degrees, having to glue all the objects on the table, secure them to prevent them from falling down. And at that moment you realise that what you have seen is just a perspective game.

RS: And actor Luca Argentero, who plays Leonardo in the movie, is particularly touching when he says that famous sentence 'In verità vi dico, qualcuno mi tradirà' ('I tell you, one of you will betray me').

JGL: We worked a lot with Professor Marani on this scene, and we came up with the idea of putting Leonardo in the centre of the universe and everything surrounding him, not necessarily as Jesus himself but as the creator.

When you are doing cinema, there are some moments that become magical and that you will remember forever as a director, when everything is at the right place and at the right moment. When, at the end of the scene, Luca said those words and looked at the camera, it was so powerful that when I said 'Cut', ending the scene, everyone from the production stood there still, everyone, maybe for a minute, maybe longer, you could almost hear a deep sigh, and I believe you can feel it on the screen.

RS: Who do you think the real Leonardo was?

JGL: I think the real Leonardo da Vinci had several faces, you can only understand him looking through the chamber of mirrors, he was an incredibly curious person, observant, funny, talented, not affectionate, a storm of ideas; one of his goals was to be recognised. I believe he was more similar to us than one might believe. He was also the product of an era, of his time, he was the best idea of a Renaissance man, he could be an engineer and an architect, an artist, a poet, which is very different from what we are used to now. In the Renaissance era, the man was the centre of the universe, and he truly believed he was at the centre of the universe.

Leonardo in his own words

Leonardo and the creation of his icon can be found in different aspects of his life. He was so smart, he had an opinion on everything, and that is reflected in his own words, words that have been shared by many and keep being shared on social media, representing the society of the time as well as the current one. He had a point of view, an approach, a different thought on every single thing and every aspect of life. He could be incredibly introspective, even more so in the last years of his life, he was a man who would just keep feelings, passions to himself, yet his notes show that some of his deepest thoughts and considerations have been extracted; the following quotes, disseminated, often endlessly on social media, keep adding to his status as one of the most interesting icons of our time.

Leonardo on painting and poetry

Leonardo naturally had several thoughts when it came to painting and art; the following quotes particularly deal with the idea of painting seen as poetry, the sfumato and the concept of art as never being quite finished.

'Painting is poetry that is seen rather than felt, and poetry is painting that is felt rather than seen.'

'A painter should begin every canvas with a wash of black because all things in nature are dark except where exposed by the light.'

'The painter has the universe in his mind and hands.'

'Art is never finished, only abandoned.'

Leonardo on flying

Leonardo was fascinated by flight and by the movement of birds, he could look at them for days. Flying would have been his biggest dream.

'Once you have tasted flight, you will forever walk the Earth with your eyes turned skyward, for there you have been, and there you will always long to return.'

Leonardo on studying

Leonardo was a lifetime student and he could hardly imagine a life without learning or exploring something new.

'Study without desire spoils the memory, and it retains nothing that it takes in.'

'One can have no smaller or greater mastery than mastery of oneself.'

'Learning never exhausts the mind.'

Leonardo on being a vegetarian

Leonardo was a vegetarian; he would only eat what his cook Mathurine would make for him, usually vegetable soups. He was very strong in his position when it came to being a vegetarian and would compare eating animals to murder.

'I have from an early age abjured the use of meat, and the time will come when men such as I will look upon the murder of animals as they now look upon the murder of men.'

Leonardo's philosophy

Was Leonardo a philosopher? He was. He most certainly questioned life on a regular basis, and it is no surprise that he decided to express himself on several topics from knowledge to death. It is in his quotes, which echo a more philosophical approach to life, that it is interesting to note Leonardo's personality and glimpses of what a positive force he was. It is apparent that he was not a man who liked to plan in advance, but who was mindful enough to live in the moment. In his personal notes, he often speaks of how to achieve happiness and how that is often related to being in a position of spending time learning and understanding what's around us.

'I love those who can smile in trouble.'

'Nothing can be loved or hated unless it is first understood.'

'The knowledge of all things is possible.'

'I have been impressed with the urgency of doing. Knowing is not enough; we must apply. Being willing is not enough; we must do.'

'There are three classes of people: those who see. Those who see when they are shown. Those who do not see.'

Leonardo on the human body

The *Vitruvian Man* was one of the most important works by Leonardo and it is a true testimony to his extensive study of the human body, particularly concerning proportions. It is something that was the product of endless studies and researches on the human body and how it worked. Yet despite such a scientific approach, he never became cynical when it comes to human beings; he was genuinely interested in understanding how everything worked but that did not make him a sceptic when it came to human beings; as a result of this, some of his quotes about the human body succeed in assuming scientific yet somewhat poetic sentiments.

It is particularly interesting to note what he says about the soul and how it's imprisoned in the human body, something that echoes his Catholic background and a religion that, despite being covered under a pile of scientific studies and years of questioning everything he knew, was still incredibly present in his life, perhaps much more so as he got older.

'The function of muscle is to pull and not to push, except in the case of the genitals and the tongue.'

'The eye is the window of the human body through which it feels its way and enjoys the beauty of the world.'

'I have found that in the composition of the human body as compared with the bodies of animals, the organs of sense are duller and coarser. Thus, it is composed of less ingenious instruments, and of spaces less capacious for receiving the faculties of sense.'

'The soul is content to stay imprisoned in the human body... for through the eyes all the various things of nature are represented to the soul.'

Leonardo on death

As he got a bit more nostalgic, he was found questioning death and perhaps his whole life.

'I thought I was learning to live; I was only learning to die.'

Leonardo on bravery

Was Leonardo a brave man? He was a man who did not shy away from adventure and would move literally anywhere for work reasons, yet he was also prone to feelings of insecurity.

'I love those who can smile in trouble, who can gather strength from distress, and grow brave by reflection.'

Leonardo on dreams

What did Leonardo dream of? Money? Success? Love? He probably dreamt of being accepted by the society of the time, finding a patron who would support him and his inventions extensively and without asking for much in return; someone who would perhaps believe in him.

'Why does the eye see a thing more clearly in dreams than with the imagination being awake?'

Leonardo on understanding

He believed in the 'joy' of understanding. He would spend time writing, analysing or looking at life from a different perspective, a point of view no one else had explored before. Emotions were not something he felt comfortable with, so everything we have of Leonardo was pure and simple science.

'The noblest pleasure is the joy of understanding.'

Leonardo on wisdom

At the end of his days, he was a man of wisdom, he was a man who had lived and experienced many and different things and he carried that particular wisdom and depth in his eyes and in his background.

'Wisdom is the daughter of experience.'

It is in his writing that glimpses of Leonardo can be traced, tracked, and maybe understood: his thoughts, his research, his opinions, that's where they are, where we can have a look at his most personal thoughts. Leonardo was an introspective man, a man whose consciousness led him to unveil some of the most interesting scientific discoveries, a man who was smart, sensitive and who left us some precious insights concerning his works, paintings and elaborate research and inventions.

Could the real Leonardo hide behind these notes? Or was he in the paintings he made? Was he in his engineering efforts? Was he in his incessant study of botany? Was he in the tales of those who had known him? Was he in the representations of his life and work?

Who was the real Leonardo? He was a funny man, a man of irony, a man who painted but didn't like to be defined or even labelled as a painter. He was an engineer and a very good one. He was a man of science, a man who didn't often feel as if he was in the right place. He was a man who had to fight for a position within the society of the time, someone who was human and could not help but be jealous of his peers. He was a pioneer, there is no question about that. He was probably too advanced for his age, for his time and for his own artistry. He was a man who enjoyed looking at life from a perspective that was often misjudged, a man who was sensitive enough to paint beautiful angels and scientific enough to open cadavers, dissect them and find out how everything worked, where we originated from, where we came from and how everything functioned.

He was unpredictable, his mind was quick but he was not constant and he could hardly bring himself to finish anything, no matter what it was. His own projects were too outrageous, scary and dangerous, and he could rarely find patrons who would be open to embracing his bravery.

He was a man, a lover, someone who experienced love, could talk about love but did not necessarily like to do so. He did not enjoy expressing love in his works, in his sketches. He saw love in the eyes of others, and perhaps something about its power must have frightened him, something that would have put him at the mercy of someone else; he witnessed this kind of love in his paintings and his portraits.

He was a man who had to deal with power, brutality and war. He had patrons, princes and was often commissioned. Leonardo was a rebel, someone who didn't like being told what to do, how to do it and for how long, he could not have a timescale. He was a free thinker, a researcher, someone who would research and write and question everything. He was a town planner, he was a singer, he was a party planner, someone who would create the most beautiful, spectacular scenography for different festivals at court.

He was a writer; he wrote and wrote, notes, long pages, and words about science, geometry, medicine, the world, words about life, his life: a life spent researching things, researching people, researching the world. He wrote words often abruptly stopped by sketches: a face, a life, a narrative he had been attracted to, charmed by, something that had caught his eye while walking down the street. He was a competitor, a friend, someone who always predicted and anticipated the future, a celestial being, someone who 'woke up too soon', according to Freud.

And then he was a son, a nephew, a grandson, an icon, a polymath as many defined him, the *Mona Lisa*'s painter. He was a mystery, a narrative, valid today like yesterday, and then he became human, he became us.

Bibliography

Books and articles consulted

Abbott, E. *A History of Celibacy*. Simon and Schuster, 2000.

Belliotti, R. *Niccolò Machiavelli: The Laughing Lion and the Strutting Fox*. Lexington Books, 2010.

Burke, P. *The Italian Renaissance: Culture and Society in Italy*. Polity Press, 1986.

Brown, D. *The Da Vinci Code*. Doubleday Transworld & Bantam Books, 2003.

Ettlinger, Helen S. *Visibilis et Invisibilis: The Mistress in Italian Renaissance Court Society*. Cambridge University Press, 1994.

Forey, A. *Military Orders and Crusades*. Ashgate Publishing Limited, 1994.

Freud, S. *Leonardo*. Pelican Books, 1963.

Gadol, J.K. 'Did Women Have a Renaissance?' in R. Bridenthal and C. Koonz, *Becoming Visible: Women in European History*. Houghton Mifflin, 1977.

Kreft, T. & Lohrmann, D. *Leonardo da Vinci's Design for the Construction of Burning Mirrors*. Franz Steiner Verlag, 2020.

Isaacson, W. *Leonardo da Vinci: The Biography*. Simon and Schuster, 2017.

Isbouts, J. & Heath Brown, C. *The Da Vinci Legacy*. Apollo Publishers, 2019.

Masters, R.D. *Machiavelli, Leonardo and the Science of Power*. University of Notre Dame Press, 1996.

Vasari, G. *The Life of Leonardo da Vinci*. Translated by Martin Kemp. Thames and Hudson, 2019.

Richter, J.P. (translator). *The Notebooks of Leonardo da Vinci*. Pacific Publishing Studio, 2010.

Rocke, M. *Forbidden Friendships*. Oxford University Press, 1996.

Symonds, J.A. *Renaissance in Italy: The Age of the Despots, Volume I*. Smith, Elder & Co., 1877.

Strathern, P. *The Artist, the Philosopher and the Warrior*. Penguin Random House, 2009.

Thompson, B. *Humanists and Reformers: A History of the Renaissance and Reformation*. William B. Eerdmans Publishing Company, 1996.

Vahland, K. *The Da Vinci Women: The Untold Feminist Power of Leonardo's Art*. Hachette, 2020.

Vinceti, S. *Il Segreto della Gioconda*. Armando Editore, 2018.

Pictures

Cover Picture by Natata
Back Cover by Mauromod
Lucky Red Pictures: from the film *Io Leonardo* – a production by Sky and Progetto Immagine
© foto Fabio Zayed e Maila Iacovelli

Illustrations

Mona Lisa mask, sanitiser: Photo by Yaroslav Danylchenko from Pexels
Balloon: Image by DarkWorkX from Pixabay
Mona Lisa: Image by 3444753 from Pixabay
Last Supper: Image by 3444753 from Pixabay

Films

Da Vinci's Demons: BBC Worldwide Productions, Phantom Four Films.
Io Leonardo, a production by Sky and Progetto Immagine. Distributed by Lucky Red.
Ulisse, Il piacere della scoperta. Leonardo da Vinci. Rai 1. Radiotelevisione Italiana Spa.

Websites consulted

adsabs.harvard.edu/full/2008POBeo..85..213D
airandspace.si.edu/stories/editorial/leonardo-da-vinci-and-flight

Bibliography

aparchive.com/metadata/youtube/923f0a752d88b2907288773da5108a2d

artsy.net/news/artsy-editorial-scientists-solved-mystery-glass-orb-salvator-mundi

artsy.net/news/artsy-editorial-second-portrait-leonardo-da-vinci-discovered

azquotes.com/author/15101-Leonardo_da_Vinci/tag

bbc.co.uk/history/historic_figures/da_vinci_leonardo.shtml

bbc.com/culture/story/20191107-the-men-who-leonardo-da-vinci-loved

biography.com/artist/donatello

biography.com/political-figure/lucrezia-borgia

bloomberg.com/news/features/2020-03-25/3m-doubled-production-of-n95-face-masks-to-fight-coronavirus

britannica.com/biography/Cesare-Borgia

britannica.com/biography/Donatello

britannica.com/biography/Donato-Bramante/Roman-period

britannica.com/biography/Michelangelo

britannica.com/biography/Michelangelo/The-ceiling-of-the-Sistine-Chapel

britannica.com/biography/Paulus-Jovius

britannica.com/biography/Raphael-Italian-painter-and-architect

britannica.com/biography/Sandro-Botticelli/Secular-patronage-and-works

britannica.com/topic/Guidi-family

britannica.com/topic/Platonic-Academy

businessinsider.com/leonardo-da-vinci-predictions-2019-5?r=US&IR=T

businessinsider.com/leonardo-da-vinci-predictions-2019-5?r=US&IR=T#robot-11

chateau-amboise.com/en/page-siege-de-la-cour-des-valois-aux-xve-et-xvie-siecles

curiocity.travel/curiocities/florence/leonardo-da-vinci-and-sandro-botticellis-tre-rane-inn/

dazeddigital.com/art-photography/article/41743/1/banksy-girl-with-balloon-painting-pranks-sotherbys-london

discoveringdavinci.com/letters

discoveringdavinci.com/melzi

discoveringdavinci.com/salai

drawingacademy.com/leonardo-da-vincis-pupil-salai

facebook.com/banksyamsterdam/posts/the-official-leonardo-da-vinci-exhibition-website-is-online-were-counting-down-t/583838298486325/

florenceinferno.com/gates-of-paradise/

florenceinferno.com/lorenzo-the-magnificent/

getty.edu/art/collection/artists/23985/marco-d'-oggiono-italian-about-1467-1524/

gingkoedizioni.it/caterina-leonardo-da-vincis-mother-died-in-his-arms-while-in-milan/

heconversation.com/leonardo-da-vinci-designed-an-ideal-city-that-was-centuries-ahead-of-its-time-111884

history.com/topics/middle-ages/the-knights-templar

history.com/topics/renaissance/medici-family

history.com/topics/renaissance/renaissance

historycrunch.com/milan-in-the-renaissance.html#/

historycrunch.com/venice-in-the-renaissance.html#/

historyextra.com/period/medieval/leonardo-da-vincis-genius-visions-future-sketches/

historyofroyalwomen.com/tuscany/clarice-orsini-a-roman-in-florence/

historytoday.com/archive/months-past/death-cesare-borgia

huffpost.com/entry/the-da-vinci-astronomy_b_4065100

humanism.org.uk/humanism/the-humanist-tradition/renaissance/

hyperallergic.com/162126/supposedly-hidden-from-hitler-for-its-supernatural-powers-da-vinci-goes-on-rare-public-view/

iep.utm.edu/machiave/

ilfattoquotidiano.it/2016/04/15/leonardo-da-vinci-scoperti-35-discendenti-ancora-in-vita-e-tra-loro-ce-franco-zeffirelli/2640289/

italianrenaissanceresources.com/units/unit-2/essays/husbands-and-wives/

italianrenaissanceresources.com/units/unit-2/essays/lovers-case-studies/

jpost.com/opinion/exploring-the-jewish-roots-of-leonardo-da-vinci-604860

latoscanadileonardo.it/en/places/metropolitan-city-of-florence/municipality-of-florence/palazzo-vecchio.html

leonardodavinci.net/st-john-the-baptist.jsp

loirevalley-france.co.uk/loire-valley-chateaux/chateau-le-clos-luce-leonardo-da-vinci-park louvre.fr/en/oeuvre-notices/virgin-and-child-saint-anne

louvre.fr/en/oeuvre-notices/virgin-rocks

medium.com/@jpisbouts/leonardo-da-vinci-and-the-borgias-903f0367e3e0

metmuseum.org/toah/hd/cour/hd_cour.htm

mymodernmet.com/leonardo-da-vinci-codex-atlanticus/

nationalgallery.org.uk/artists/andrea-del-verrocchio

nationalgallery.org.uk/artists/martino-piazza

nationalgallery.org.uk/paintings/learn-about-art/paintings-in-depth/mysterious-virgin?viewPage=5

news.artnet.com/art-world/jose-manuel-ballester-concealed-spaces-1814043

news.artnet.com/art-world/secrets-of-da-vincis-lady-with-an-ermine-finally-revealed-117891

news.artnet.com/art-world/true-hidden-message-da-vinci-last-supper-581756

newyorker.com/magazine/2017/10/16/the-secret-lives-of-leonardo-da-vinci

nga.gov/collection/art-object-page.134.html

nga.gov/collection/highlights/da-vinci-ginevra-de-benci.html

nga.gov/collection/artist-info.976.html

nytimes.com/1996/12/08/us/scholar-sees-leonardo-s-influence-on-machiavelli.html

nytimes.com/1999/09/14/arts/arts-abroad-leonardo-s-huge-horse-comes-to-life-500-years-later.html

oxfordbibliographies.com/view/document/obo-9780195399301/obo-9780195399301-0174.xml

pinknews.co.uk/2019/11/08/leonardo-da-vinci-sexuality-opera-alex-mills-london/

raiplay.it/video/2019/09/ulisse-il-piacere-della-scoperta---leonardo-genio-universale-91cab0ef-b592-4585-8e11-10cf98275705.html

rct.uk/collection/912353/sketches-for-the-trivulzio-monument-and-other-studies

servitefriars.org/about-us/

sothebys.com/en/articles/a-monumental-reinterpretation-of-leonardo-da-vincis-last-supper

sothebys.com/en/videos/leonardo-da-vincis-the-lady-with-an-ermine-a-beguiling-portrait-of-elegant-mystique sparknotes.com/poetry/donne/themes/

strangehistory.net/2015/04/21/gay-ponte-vecchio-and-the-office-of-the-night/

telegraph.co.uk/culture/art/art-features/10453444/Was-Michelangelo-a-better-artist-than-Leonardo-da-Vinci.html

telegraph.co.uk/news/worldnews/europe/italy/6377214/Italian-palace-fresco-may-hide-Leonardo-da-Vinci-masterpiece.html

theartstory.org/artist/banksy/artworks/

theculturetrip.com/europe/france/articles/the-unknown-life-of-leonardo-da-vinci-in-france/

theguardian.com/artanddesign/2011/oct/19/leonardo-da-vinci-lusts

thestar.com.my/lifestyle/style/2019/12/17/leonardo-da-vinci-artworks-are-fashion039s-newest-style-inspiration

theverge.com/2013/12/4/5173992/art-masterpieces-recreated-in-lego

thevintagenews.com/2018/09/01/da-vinci-weapons/

thomasnet.com/insights/meet-mona-lisa-through-the-power-of-vr-tech/

tudortimes.co.uk/guest-articles/anne-boleyn-in-france

uffizi.it/en/artworks/annunciation

vam.ac.uk/content/articles/w/women-in-the-renaissance/

vinci-closluce.com/en/place-presentation

visittuscany.com/en/time-based-tours/day-trip-vinci/